# A PICTURE OF SURREY

*Moorhouse Bank, the last group of buildings in Surrey before crossing the boundary into Kent*

# A PICTURE OF SURREY

by JOHN L. BAKER

with drawings by the author

ROBERT HALE LIMITED      LONDON

© *John L. Baker 1980*
*First published in Great Britain* 1980

ISBN  0  7091  8130  2

Robert Hale Limited
Clerkenwell House
Clerkenwell Green
London EC1R 0HT

PHOTOSET AND PRINTED
IN GREAT BRITAIN BY
REDWOOD BURN LIMITED
TROWBRIDGE, BOUND BY
KEMP HALL BINDERY, OXFORD

# Contents

| | | page |
|---|---|---|
| | *Introduction* | 13 |
| 1 | Farnham to St Catherine's | 17 |
| 2 | Guildford | 29 |
| 3 | Nonsuch Park to Merrow | 43 |
| 4 | Shalford – Albury | 61 |
| 5 | Shere – Dorking – Buckland | 73 |
| 6 | Reigate to the Borders of Kent | 87 |
| 7 | Banstead to Gatton | 99 |
| 8 | Farleigh to Burstow | 113 |
| 9 | River Wey | 123 |
| 10 | The Portsmouth Road | 143 |
| 11 | The Heathland Villages of North-West Surrey | 157 |
| 12 | The River Thames | 171 |
| 13 | River Mole | 185 |
| 14 | Stane Street | 197 |
| | *Glossary* | 209 |
| | *Bibliography* | 217 |
| | *Index* | 219 |

COMPANION VOLUMES

*Heart of England* by Louise Wright and James Priddey
*Rural Kent* by John Boyle and John L. Berbiers
*Cotswold Heritage* by Louise Wright and James Priddey
*Sussex Scenes* by Michael H. C. Baker
*Somerset Scenes* by Aylwin Sampson

# Illustrations

|  | page |
| --- | --- |
| Moorhouse Bank | 2 |
| Details of structure | 12 |
| Bishop Waynflete's Tower, Farnham Castle | 16 |
| Willmer House | 19 |
| Waverley Abbey | 20 |
| No. 58 The Street, Puttenham | 23 |
| Puttenham Priory | 24 |
| The great barn of Wanborough | 25 |
| Watts Chapel | 26 |
| White Hart Cottage, Compton | 27 |
| The group of buildings known as Castle Arch | 28 |
| The Norman keep of Guildford Castle | 29 |
| St Mary's Church, Quarry Street, Guildford | 31 |
| The Guildhall, Guildford | 32 |
| George Abbot's Hospital | 34 |
| Guildford House | 35 |
| Guildford's Royal Grammar School | 37 |
| The Corona Restaurant, Guildford | 38 |
| Caleb Lovejoy Almshouses | 39 |
| The modern cathedral on Stag Hill, Guildford | 41 |
| Princes Stand, Epsom Downs | 44 |
| Sweech House, Leatherhead | 46 |
| No. 33 Church Street, Leatherhead | 47 |
| St Mary's Church, Fetcham | 48 |
| Polesden Lacey | 49 |
| The garden front of Horsley Towers | 51 |
| The Manor House, East Horsley | 52 |
| The Old Cottage, West Horsley | 53 |
| St Mary's Church, West Horsley | 54 |
| Tunmore Cottage, East Clandon | 55 |
| The church of St Peter and St Paul, West Clandon | 56 |
| Clandon Park | 57 |
| The Marble Hall at Clandon Park | 58 |
| The Hunting Room, Clandon Park | 59 |
| Shalford Mill | 60 |
| The Grantley Arms, Wonersh | 63 |

The Dower House, Wonersh 64
Watts Cottage, Shamley Green 65
Barnett Farm 66
Chilworth Manor 68
Cookes Place, Albury 70
The old church of St Peter and St Paul, Albury 71
Shere Church and a Wealden house 72
King John House 75
Malthouse Cottages 76
Crossways Farmhouse, Abinger 78
Wotton Church 79
St Barnabas's Church on Ranmore 81
St Martin's, Dorking 82
Buckland Green 85
The old Town Hall, Reigate 86
Brownes Lodge, Reigate 88
Nutfield Church 89
Bletchingley 91
The White Hart, Godstone 92
The Bell Inn, Oxted 94
Limpsfield 97
Woodmans Cottage, Banstead 98
Banstead Wood 100
Tadworth Court 101
Chipstead Church 102
Chaldon Church 106
Quality Street, Merstham 109

The Town Hall, Gatton 110
Puttenden Manor 112
Farleigh Church 114
Haxted Mill 117
Lingfield 118
The Guest Hall, Lingfield 119
Burstow Church 121
The post-mill at Outwood 122
Byfleet Manor House 125
Newark Priory 126
St Nicholas's Church, Pyrford 127
Woking Palace 128
The Old Manor House, Old Woking 129
Old Woking Church from Church Street 129
The old Brew House, Old Woking 130
Little Pittance, Smithwood Common 132
Cranleigh Church 133
Alford House 134
Alford 135
Oak Tree Cottage 136
The Crown Inn, Chiddingfold 138
Unstead Farm 139
Eashing Bridge 140
Peper Harow Granary 142
St George's Church, Esher 143
Waynflete's Tower, Esher 144
Claremont 145

The Anchor, Ripley 147
Ripley 148
Loseley House 151
The Town Hall, Godalming 152
Step Cottages, Witley 153
Hill Farm, Thursley 155
Cosford Mill 156
Roman ruins at Virginia Water 158
Redlands Farm 159
Botleys Park 161
The Mosque at Woking 162
Pirbright Church 163
Merrist Wood, Worplesdon 164
Whites Farm, Worplesdon 167
Ash Church and Hartshorn Cottage 168
Stanwell Church 170
Chertsey Bridge 174
Curfew House, Chertsey 175
The Cedars, Chertsey 177
The Manor House, Walton 178

Walton Church 180
The Shannon Monument, Walton Church 183
The Bell Inn, East Molesey 184
Ham Manor, Cobham 186
Stoke D'Abernon Church 187
One of the small cottages at Patchesham 188
Leatherhead Bridge 189
Castle Mill, Dorking 191
Church Street, Betchworth 192
Greens Farm, Newdigate 195
Juniper Hall 196
St Michael's Church, Mickleham 199
Mile House, Dorking 200
Pollingfold 203
Ewhurst 204
The Swallow Tile Works 205
Cobbetts, Forest Green 206
The Hallams near Wonersh 207

Surrey (map) 14

# Acknowledgments

Many friends have given me their time and valuable advice unstintingly. I particularly thank those who have read my manuscript.

Some material from my drawings and articles published in The *Surrey Advertiser* has been used, and I wish to thank Mr E.W. Adams, the editor, for his encouragement and enthusiasm for my subject.

I also thank owners for permission to reproduce drawings now in private collections.

Most of the buildings mentioned are private property, but, wherever I have been, people have welcomed me into their homes. I have, therefore, been able to examine almost every house in great detail, including the roof where necessary. I am deeply grateful for this privilege and wish to stress that the privacy of owners must be respected at all times, the mention of a house in this book does not necessarily mean that it is open to the public.

For advice and practical help in presenting my work for publication I thank Miss Tessa Cockett, who with the assistance of Miss Mary Bishop, took on the arduous task of deciphering and typing my manuscript.

Finally I thank my wife for bearing with me and sustaining me over a long period of intensive work and travel.

To the memory of my parents

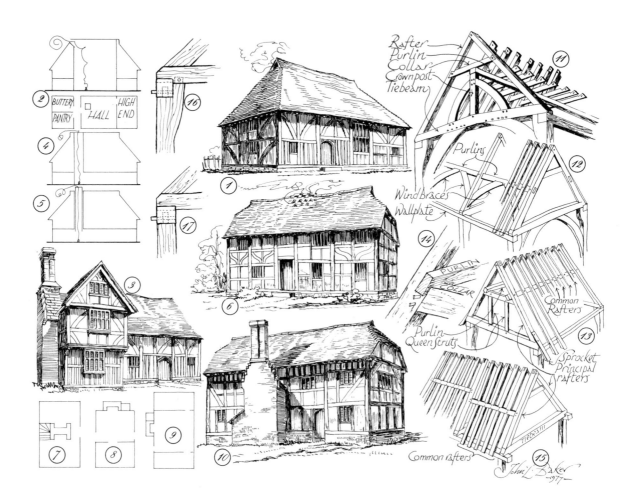

② BUTTERY PANTRY · HALL · HIGH END

④

⑤

⑯

⑰

①

③

⑥

⑦

⑧

⑨

⑩

Rafter
Purlin
Collar
Crownpost
Tiebeam

⑪

⑫

Purlins

Windbraces
Wallplate

⑭

PURLIN

COLLAR

Purlin
Queen Struts

Common
Rafters

⑬

Sprocket
Principal
Rafters

Tiebeam

Common rafters

⑮

John L. Baker
1977

# Introduction

The history of Surrey is bound up in the roads that traverse it, which link important centres outside its boundaries; the county never had a large centre of population on which routes converged.

The route from west to east across the North Downs is of great antiquity and linked the West Country with the Channel ports.

Roads from north to south were always difficult. The gaps in the Downs at Guildford, Dorking and Caterham provided ways through the hills, but the heavy clay of the Weald was always a hazard. Roman Stane Street cut across the Weald, but medieval roads generally shunned the difficulty of crossing the intractable clay of the western part.

The hypothesis could be advanced that there is a link between the easier, ancient west-east route and the transmission of architectural ideas—at the vernacular level—across the county from Hampshire to Kent.

Evidence points to this in the use of the side purlin roof. It had reached a high stage of development in Hampshire by the early fifteenth century, it occurred in Surrey about 1480, and then in Kent in the late sixteenth century.

The southward movement of ideas is not observable until the seventeenth century when the use of the butted side purlin, into which are butted common rafters, is seen to spread out from London. A decorative brick style, frequently associated with this roof form, also came to Surrey via London at this time.

A standard vernacular house type had become established in south-east England by 1300, and is shown in (1). Based upon the hall, with an open hearth for heating, the plan remained unchanged in its essentials until the mid-sixteenth century (2).

The number of bays—structural divisions or units—to each section varied, but the usual plan had a two-bay hall with single bays at each end. The master's parlour—high end, and the service end—buttery and pantry, had upper rooms. In a small house of only two bays the service and parlour could be combined in one bay with a 'bower', or sleeping place, above the service room.

There was always a front and back door opposite each other at the service end of the hall, or sometimes just within the service end. A screen was used to form a passage across the house between these doors, alternatively, there were two short wings, or speres, to screen the en-

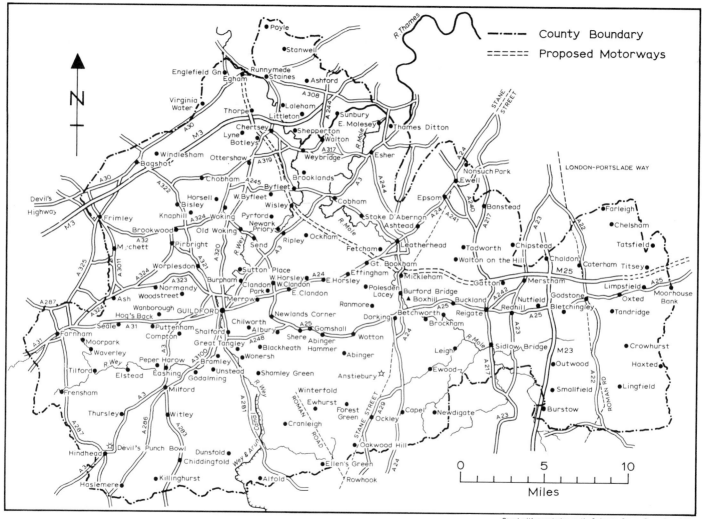

trances. The treatment varied according to the importance of the house. A high survival rate of this feature in many houses, even after they had ceased to be open halls, suggests that it had a social significance deeply rooted in past usage.

A crosswing could be an integral part of the original building, or it could be a later addition as in (3).

With changes in social attitudes away from the communal life in an open hall in the mid-sixteenth century, the need arose for more separate rooms in a house. An upper room was created by inserting a floor in the hall, a narrow section being left open to form a shaft, or smoke bay (4). Later, a brick chimney was often constructed within the smoke bay (5).

New houses were built with smoke bays (6), or later, with brick chimneys placed centrally (7), or at one end (8).

In the seventeenth century many houses had chimneys built on the long side of the house (9) and (10). The stairs in such houses were often in a stair turret placed alongside the stack.

Roof construction followed a distinct process of development. The earliest form had no longitudinal support,

i.e. purlins. Examples may be seen in many churches such as the chancel at Compton.

Transverse bracing was used in early roofs, in particular scissor braces, that, as the name implies, crossed between pairs of rafters, e.g. St Mary's, Guildford. Long braces parallel to the rafters that crossed as they passed from the principal posts to the opposite rafters, i.e. Old Court Cottage, Limpsfield, and The Forge, Dunsfold, were also used.

The crownpost structure provided a centre purlin (11). This was followed by the use of a side purlin (12) butted between principal rafters.

Then followed the through side purlin clasped by a collar (13), a later sixteenth-century modification used a reducing principal rafter (14). This latter form being frequently associated with smoke-bay houses.

Butted side purlins not in line, with common rafters butted into them (15), came in the 1630s and continued in use until the eighteenth century, although by then purlins were often butted in line.

A useful indicator of date is the jowl (16), it is not found in very early work, or in work after the early years of the seventeenth century (17).

*Bishop Waynflete's great tower of brick at Farnham Castle, a palace of the Bishops of Winchester until modern times*

# CHAPTER ONE

# Farnham to St Catherine's

The route across Surrey from west to east, sometimes called the Hoar Way before it enters the county west of Farnham, has been romantically called the Pilgrims' Way. This idea was promoted in the nineteenth century and given credence by Captain Edward Renouard James, R.E., so naming the route on the Ordnance Survey map in the 1860s.

Some pilgrims may well have used the route, as did many other travellers, but its real importance is that it was used by man from the very earliest times. The exact route, whether up on the Downs or below in the valley, has been disputed, but the general line is now represented by the North Downs Way and the A25.

The first town in Surrey that this ancient route enters is Farnham. Small and compact, its buildings retain the scale and proportion of more elegant days. Brick predominates, for the town reached a zenith of prosperity when brick houses were the height of fashion. Indeed, such was the

social value of living in such a house that some timber-framed houses were fronted in brick, thereby satisfying the need to keep up with the trend.

Georgian brick the town may be, in appearance, but it undoubtedly retains a feeling of medieval cosiness from the symbolically protective castle on the hill above it. The hill was probably fortified in Saxon times, but in 1138 the Norman, Henry de Blois, Bishop of Winchester and brother of King Stephen, built there a shell keep placed upon a motte created by earth thrown up from a surrounding ditch. Later, in the twelfth century, the domestic range of the castle was extended to include a great hall and chapel.

The plan of the great twelfth-century aisled hall of Farnham Castle can be easily identified. The cross passage remains with the usual three entrances out of it to the service end, the middle opening of the three being larger and unusually elaborate with lovely twelfth-century detail. This door leads to the detached kitchen, still identifiable as the building beyond, but it has been suggested that it was particularly elaborate because it also gave access to the chapel. Most exciting of all is a survival from the great hall, a wooden arcade post with simple carved capital. It is still in place, but in a recess now used as a cupboard.

Of the later additions, the most significant are the brick tower (1470–5), by Bishop Waynflete of Winchester and the galleried range of lodgings, of about 1550, to the north-west of the inner court. Bishop Waynflete's tower was the first important brick building in Surrey. The work was superbly executed, and survives little altered except for the insertion of later sash-windows which, unfortunately, break across the diaper pattern in the brickwork.

The castle was damaged during the Civil War and in the later seventeenth century the great hall was considerably modified, a new staircase was placed to the east of it, and a new chapel fitted with woodcarving of the kind always attributed to Grinling Gibbons—but on this occasion with some justification.

In the town below the castle there is a remarkable collection of fine houses, many of the eighteenth and early nineteenth centuries. There are also many of much earlier date, some often now difficult to identify from the street as they stand behind brick fronts grafted on to them in the eighteenth century to conform to fashion.

Farnham Church is an important feature of the town although it was unfortunately severely restored in 1855 by B. Ferrey. The large tower, originally of the fifteenth century and now with nineteenth-century battlements and pinnacles, clearly contributes to the townscape. William Cobbett, author of *Rural Rides*, was born in Farnham, and is buried in the churchyard.

Of the eighteenth-century houses in the town, Willmer House in West Street has one of the best brick façades in the county. It is comparable with work in London. The doorcase, with an upward cusping of the architrave, is very similar to another in Buckingham Street, Strand.

All early records of the house have gone: it is not known who built it or who commissioned it, and it is only upon the recollection of someone who remembered once seeing the lost deeds that it is believed that the original cost was £523—in 1723—when it was sold by a John Thorpe. The initials 'J.T.' and the date 1718 on the rainwater heads appear to give this story credence.

Willmer House was acquired by Farnham Council in 1960. It now houses the Farnham Museum collections which have been built up over the last eighteen years or so with an emphasis on local interests. There are mementoes and objects once owned by such local men as William Cobbett, the clockmaker Avenell, and the painter Stephen Elmer. Also, there is a collection of drawings by the architect, Harold Falkner.

A little to the west of Willmer House is Sandford House, said to have been built by John Mainwaring in 1757.

No. 41 West Street has a frieze with rondels and a blind brick arcade divides the ground floor. This is genuine, of about 1775, but No. 40 nearby is not: it is an almost indistinguishable reproduction by Harold Falkner.

Falkner was an outstanding character and he undoubtedly exerted—should I say imposed—a beneficial influ-

*Willmer House at Farnham, one of the finest brick façades in the county, probably built by a London craftsman in about 1718*

*Waverley Abbey, the first Cistercian foundation in England, and probably the inspiration for the title of Sir Walter Scott's Waverley novels*

ence on Farnham in the 1930s. Although Falkner lived until 1963, he really belonged to the generation of architects before the First World War. He knew such men as Norman Shaw, Walter Crane, Ernest Gimson and Sir Edwin Lutyens, and was also a nephew of that remarkable lady, Gertrude Jekyll.

He was involved mainly with private housing, some of it speculative, and with a little restoration and conversion work. In 1901 the idea of a garden suburb at Great Austins, to the south of Farnham, was put forward. Falkner was involved and built about 50 of the 150 houses. He also built the Town Hall at the corner of Castle Street and the Borough, and he restored the Bailiffs' Hall of 1674 which was in a decorative brick style popular in Surrey in the mid-seventeenth century—a style that can be seen at its best at Crossways Farm, Abinger.

At the lower end of Castle Street, a small market is still held on the site of the old Market House that stood until 1866 and which is believed to have been built in the mid-sixteenth century. Other buildings once here were the Corn Exchange, a Gothic Revival building by E. Wyndham Tarn built in the 1860s, and John and James Knight's Farnham Bank, designed by Norman Shaw.

Shaw's bank was in an Elizabethan style, timber-framed and over-large in Shaw's way of producing a dramatic effect. Falkner may have been aware of the unsuitable scale of Shaw's bank, but his part in its destruction must have caused him much heart-searching for he was an admirer of Shaw and was greatly influenced by him in his own work.

Apart from his restoration work, Falkner began the development of his own Dippenhall estate in the 1920s and this continued until his death. Although original in outlook, he became more and more eccentric as he grew older. Burles Lodge was one of his last houses and remained unfinished at his death. After years of neglect it has been bought by a builder sympathetic towards Falkner, and who has the time to finish it.

Beyond Farnham the road rises up to the spine of the Hog's Back, where the chalk ridge is at its narrowest—a small piece of Surrey where one is always conscious of the sky and the weather.

To the south of the western end of the ridge, hidden in a valley, is the forlorn ruin of Waverley Abbey. The site seems remote even now, but how much more so must it have been in 1128 when William Giffard, Bishop of Winchester, founded the abbey—the first Cistercian house in Britain.

Waverley was endowed with a tract of land through which the River Wey serpentines in wide, lazy loops. Flooding was a problem, and on occasions, alarming; the result is that the valley has silted up and the original floor levels of the twelfth century are now some six feet below present levels.

It is probable that the abbey was built in stone very

shortly after its foundation in 1128, but it was on a small scale. Larger buildings were soon required for the rapidly growing Order and a new church was begun in 1203 and dedicated in 1278. At the same time alterations were made to other buildings.

Although the rule of poverty seems to have been adhered to, the abbey must have had considerable farming interests in Surrey as well as in neighbouring counties. However, the abbey's annual revenue at the Suppression was only £174 8s 3½d. and it fell with the lesser monasteries, of £200 or less value, under the Dissolution Act of 1535–6.

The site was immediately granted to Sir William Fitzwilliam, treasurer of the King's Household, afterwards Earl of Southampton.

It is recorded that in the seventeenth century "the monastic remains underwent great dilapidations". In 1725 they were sold to Mr Child of Guildford for £13,000 and he built a house there—not on the site of the abbey, but above it where the present house stands.

The principal abbey ruins are now in the care of the Department of the Environment.

Moor Park, a little to the south of Waverley, was the home of the Temple family and is also associated with Jonathan Swift, secretary to the diplomat, Sir William Temple.

Once called Compton Hall, Moor Park was renamed by Sir William Temple who bought it around 1680. At this time it was a brick house in the Dutch style—like the Dutch house at Kew. All that can now be seen of Temple's old house is contained above the entrance of the present building where the old front door with Wren-type pedimented doorcase is surmounted with Temple's coat of arms in painted Wealden cast iron.

Extensive alterations to the house occurred in the mid-eighteenth century when the old house was encased in stucco and given a neo-classical look. The stairwell is the most attractive of these changes; it is decorated in blue and white plasterwork with delicate swags framing cherubs and musical instruments.

Successive owners eventually gave up the struggle to maintain the house in later years until, in 1948, it was condemned to demolition. However, Canon R. E. Parsons and Sir Henry Brittain wanted to use the house as a college for adult education, and with the help of Harold Falkner this was achieved.

Falkner was the first to suspect that the old house existed encased in the eighteenth-century stucco. Then drawings of the house and garden made in 1690 were discovered and these helped to establish his belief.

Further westwards is the village of Seale. Its setting is quite lovely, but the buildings are only attractive collectively. One house, East End Farm, a little out of the village, is old—about sixteenth century. The church was virtually rebuilt during the restoration by Croft in 1861–73, and there is little old work remaining except the wooden south porch, perhaps of the fifteenth century, and a monument or two.

The lane out of Seale, eastwards, pleasantly winds its way to Puttenham and passes Shoelands. Built in brick in 1616, the present house replaces a very ancient building that stood a little to the south-west, "behind a ditch" as it was described in a thirteenth-century document. Inside is a really fine original seventeenth-century stair.

The lane from Shoelands leads to Puttenham and a view over the village soon opens out. The long village street with its cottages and old farmhouses leads the eye across rising ground to complete the picture with the church tower standing amid trees.

There are buildings of all periods in Puttenham, but I have never seen a better combination of styles that also includes modern work. The village has several terraced rows including Yew Tree Cottages, Jasmine and July Cottages, and Nos. 78, 76 and 74. These are scattered throughout the village and assist in the creation of an overall impression of unity.

The oldest houses are Winter Farm, Rosemary Cottage and Old Cottage which all have fifteenth-century origins.

Street Farm is later, sixteenth century, and has barn conversions at the rear. These, together with the more recent conversion of the oasthouses near Priory Farmhouse, are

*No. 58 The Street, Puttenham, a sixteenth-century timber-framed house that was encased in Bargate stone and brick perhaps in 1685 only 100 years after it was built. The wing to the right is an eighteenth-century addition*

23

important as this form of re-use may prove to be the only future that many old farm buildings have. I feel that these conversions lack an understanding and deep love of vernacular work, an essential quality for success in this field.

Later houses add much to the village and, in particular, include No. 58 The Street which, although it has an early sixteenth-century frame, was refronted in 1685. There

*Puttenham Priory is a perfect example of a late eighteenth-century country gentleman's house, although the front conceals an earlier structure*

are also Priory Farmhouse, Home Farmhouse and to the south of the church the handsome Puttenham Priory. This has a 1762 façade showing Adamesque detail that was placed in front of an earlier stone and brick house. The architect is unknown.

The oldest work in the church is the Norman north arcade, but the tower, so important to the appearance of the village, is fifteenth century. A fire seriously damaged the church in 1735 and John Hassel's drawings of the 1820s show it after restoration with a two-decker pulpit and box pews. In 1868 a further, and now much-regretted, restoration was done by Woodyer under the direction of the Reverend W. Duckworth, a devotee of the Camden Society.

On the northern flank of the Hog's Back, opposite Puttenham, is Wanborough which is now a cluster of farm cottages, a seventeenth-century brick house, a tiny church and a series of barns. One of these barns is for me quite the most impressive building in the whole of Surrey and there can be little doubt that this magnificent structure was built by the monks of Waverley.

It is of seven bays with aisles and an outshot at the western end. The roof is a crownpost construction, and in my drawing, made from the western outshot looking east, one of the original roof trusses may be seen almost in its entirety. It shows early features such as the absence of jowls on the arcade posts, the crownposts have no downward braces to the tiebeam, and there are long passing braces from the tiebeam to the wall posts.

Four of the great aisle posts are re-used timber. Three are from a much earlier building and carry evidence of the use of a notched lap joint—a carpentry joint of the thirteenth century or earlier. The fourth post is of octagonal section and was put in as a later replacement aisle post. It has not been possible to identify the origin or age of this timber.

Sections of the aisles date to later re-builds: work at the north and south-east is mid-seventeenth century and at the south-west, including the western outshot, it is eighteenth century.

The eastern end was hipped originally, as is the western end, and clear evidence for this is given by the survival in the roof of the gablet collar. The alteration was probably done in the seventeenth or eighteenth centuries at times when other changes were made. It is very probable that in the seventeenth century extensive repairs were undertaken as parts of the internal structure appear to have suffered a long period of neglect and weathering consistent with being roofless.

Wanborough Manor, the seventeenth-century house near the barn, has a brick front in a version of the decorative brick style of the period, but rather more restrained than usual. During the Second World War the house was used as a training centre for people who worked behind

*The great barn of Wanborough that was probably built by the monks of Waverley to store produce from their outlying granges*

the enemy lines in Occupied Europe.

Also a part of the group is the little St Bartholomew Church. It is thirteenth century and was in disuse for a long period until a sympathetic restoration took place in 1862.

*Watts Chapel stands near the Watts Gallery and was built under the direction of Mrs Watts in a style evoking her own mystic symbolism*

From Wanborough the road across the Hog's Back now runs into Guildford along the Farnham road which was improved as a turnpike in 1758. This bypassed the steep descent down The Mount, the original route into the town, which is now a bridlepath coming in from the eastern end of the Hog's Back at Guildown.

East of Puttenham Church, near the Jolly Farmer and the lovely eighteenth-century Heath Cottage, is an ancient track now followed by the North Downs Way. This passes under the A3 near Limnerslease, once the home of G. F. Watts, the artist. Near here also is Watts Gallery, and the Watts Chapel that was built and decorated under the direction of Mrs Watts in a mixture of Celtic and Art Nouveau styles. The small interior of the chapel is claustrophobic with a surfeit of painted gesso decoration that is, for me, both affecting and incomprehensible.

Beyond the chapel is the village of Compton which has an ancient church of particular interest—St Nicholas. The tower may be of pre-Conquest origin and has a good shingled broach spire. The chancel is unusual as it was remodelled in the late twelfth century when an upper chapel was made above a vaulted lower sanctuary, all constructed within the existing eleventh-century walls. The western end of the upper chapel is open to the chancel and has a contemporary twelfth-century carved wooden rail. This is the earliest example of Norman carpentry in a church in the county—perhaps even in Britain. The unusual two-storeyed sanctuary remains unexplained and perhaps this also has no other extant parallel in Britain.

The nave was enlarged about 1180, a little later than the sanctuary, and has north and south arcades and a south doorway. The carving in this work shows the use of stiff-leafed foliage typical of the later work.

The village has a curving main street lined with several

cottages of early date as well as many of the nineteenth century looking as attractive as they so often can. The most notable is the fine White Hart Cottage, jettied on two sides and standing in the bank high above the road over a lower room at street level. When the house was divided into several cottages this room at the lower level was a cobbler's shop. The house is difficult to date; the roof structure, as far as it can be seen, taken together with the regular shapes in the wall framing, suggest a date around 1600.

Returning to the North Downs Way, near Limnerslease, the path runs to the north of Loseley and Littleton to join Sandy Lane which continues down to the old abandoned ferry over the River Wey at St Catherine's.

The ruined St Catherine's Chapel, built soon after 1300, is dramatically sited high above the river here. Its original form is now confused by later repairs, probably done about 1793 when the ruins were modified to improve their picturesque appearance as seen from Shalford Park, home of Robert Austen who paid for the work.

*White Hart Cottage, Compton, where a diagonal joist, or 'dragon beam', set across the corner carries the jetty as it turns from the side to the gabled end of the house*

*The group of buildings known as Castle Arch take their name from the ruined arch adjoining them,*
*built in 1256*

# CHAPTER TWO

# Guildford

There is a plaque fixed below the railings of Holy Trinity Church, Guildford, on which is written, "Eric Parker described Guildford as a beautiful city, let us keep it so".

It is obvious that this is now a mockery. To be fair, development is unavoidable, but in Guildford too many mistakes have been made, the worst of which has been to disregard the geological reasons for the town's origin by the blocking of the main route across the River Wey and by reducing the river's status to that of a ditch.

Guildford owes its existence to its position at the crossing of routes, one by land, the other by river. This crossing came at one of the few gaps in the chalk hills of the North Downs, and a settlement grew up by the river—some writers suggest on the western bank. However, the chalk spur east of the river was fortified, at least by Norman times.

The present tower keep was built in about 1125. It is one of the best of its kind in south-east England and displays a

*The once formidable Norman keep of Guildford Castle, the home of kings, now a picturesque ruin in a beautiful public flower garden*

very good use of contrasting materials. The bands of ironstone alternating with flint contrast with bargate stone used as dressings for quoins and openings.

By Henry III's time the castle had come into domestic use and was much frequented by the court. From the fourteenth century it was used increasingly as a prison, and so remained at least until sometime in the sixteenth century.

In 1611 James I granted the castle to Francis Carter who had alterations made to the keep to make it habitable.

29

These included inserting windows and a garderobe shute and these can still be seen. By 1630, however, the family had moved to Castle Arch. Now the castle keep is surrounded by a public park laid out by Henry Peak, the borough surveyor, in 1886.

The church of St Mary, in Quarry Street, was part of the town complex around the castle from the very earliest times. The tower probably pre-dates the castle as the late Saxon pilaster strips, or lesenes, confirm. There are also double splayed windows of Saxon origin in the north and south tower walls. Excavation has made it possible to conclude that west of the tower there was an aisleless nave with walls composed mostly of flint. Evidence of a timber construction of earlier date was slight.

It could be assumed that there was a chancel to the east of the tower, and about 1120 the Normans added transepts and pierced the north and south walls of the tower with arches that cut across the Saxon windows and lesenes.

In 1140 the chancel was rebuilt and some of its windows can be seen in the north and south walls of the present chancel. The existing nave was built in Transitional style about 1160–80 and, at about the same time, two apsidal chapels were added, one on either side of the chancel.

In the thirteenth century, perhaps during the first quarter, the chancel was remodelled and given a new, elegant rib vault with dog-tooth moulding supported upon clustered shafts beneath single capitals.

Somewhat later, about 1250, the aisles were widened and raised under roofs that lined up with those of the chapels. Another important addition of this time was the north doorway with its Sussex marble detached shafts and rich mouldings.

The fourteenth century contributed many windows and a piscina. In the fifteenth, more windows were put in and a rood screen which has gone: only the blocked entrance to it can be seen high up to the north of the west tower arch. It is also said that the church was re-roofed at this time and that some of the corbels in the nave were put in for this purpose.

In 1825 the eastern wall and part of the chancel were removed to widen the road. It is said that this was done at the request of the Prince Regent who offered to pay for the work, which would speed his journey to Brighton.

Apart from this, the church has suffered relatively little and the restoration by Thomas Goodchild in 1863 was not too rigorous. However, one feature has gone—the thirteenth-century painting in the north chapel revealed during the shortening of the chancel in 1825. Fortunately, Henry Prosser, a local artist, recorded it in 1836 before its total disappearance.

From the thirteenth century until the seventeenth century cloth-making was a staple industry in Surrey. Guildford, in particular, was well placed with adequate waterpower from the river to drive the fulling mills. By

*The interior of St Mary's Church, Quarry Street, the town's oldest church with Saxon work
dating to a little before the Conquest*

*The Guildhall, with its late seventeenth-century front and famous clock, is a symbol of Guildford's ancient civic pride*

the late sixteenth century the town was noted for its cloth, and the significance of this is reflected in the town's coat of arms which bears two woolsacks.

Along with trade derived from wool the town had prospered and grown. From the thirteenth century it had a Guild Merchant composed of master-craftsmen and, under the chairmanship of the mayor, it was officially responsible for keeping up the standard of trading and manufacture.

The home of the Guild Merchant—and now a symbol of the town—was the Guildhall. The front, which was built by public subscription in 1683, screens a much earlier timber-framed building at the rear which has a Tudor roof.

John Aylward is reputed to have made the great clock that projects across the High Street on a long beam. The clock is of a type common in London and is comparable to any in the City e.g. St Mary-at-Hill. In the Aylward story there is a hint of local jealousy for John Aylward was a 'foreigner'—a Londoner—and to encourage the Guild Merchant to allow him to practise his trade in Guildford he presented it with the clock. Whatever the truth of this might be, he was made a freeman.

Considerable benefit was brought to the town by George Abbot's Hospital of the Blessed Trinity which was somewhat earlier (i.e. 1619–22) in date than the Guildhall façade. George Abbot, Archbishop of Canterbury, was born in Guildford and educated at the Royal Grammar School there. His father was a weaver of modest means but George and his brothers all prospered: one became Lord Mayor of London and another Bishop of Salisbury.

In 1619–22 George Abbot built the hospital as a home for twelve old men and eight women, each with their own apartment, but with a common hall and chapel. There is a garden at the rear—similar to ones that existed behind all the High Street properties which ran down to the North Town Ditch. At a time when Inigo Jones was working in Whitehall and Greenwich introducing Italian ideas, Abbot chose to build a brick courtyard house with a great gatehouse in the manner of the early sixteenth century. He gave us the last of its kind—and also, incidentally, one of the best.

It is the perfect retreat for older people: only ten yards from the busy High Street and therefore in touch with the present, yet, once inside, peaceful and centuries removed from modern bustle.

The master and wardens of the hospital wish to extend and improve the existing accommodation of the brethren and build on the garden at the rear. There has been a heated debate concerning these proposals and at the time of writing the decision of a public enquiry is awaited.

On the first floor of the gatehouse is the council chamber with Chinese Chippendale chairs, a portrait of George Abbot by Van Somer and the hospital's Royal Charter.

Above this room is the apartment where the Duke of Monmouth was lodged on his way to London and execution in 1685.

Alongside the garden at the rear of the hospital is Cloth Hall where, in 1629, Abbot established a manufactory with an annual endowment of £100, his intention being to revitalize the cloth industry of the town by the introduction of linen and hemp weaving. The subsidy provided little incentive for the workers to make a profit and

*George Abbot's Hospital built in 1619 by George Abbot, Archbishop of Canterbury, a native of Guildford who was educated at the Royal Grammar School*

ironically Abbot possibly assisted the inevitable decay of the industry with his generosity. The project failed, in 1656 the £100 was distributed as an annual charity, and the Cloth Hall was turned into a home for paupers.

A workhouse was erected on the North Street end of Cloth Hall for Holy Trinity parish in the eighteenth century, and in the nineteenth century the hall was divided into four dwellings.

In 1856 the endowment of another benefactor was combined with Abbot's Cloth Hall fund. This was an endowment made by Thomas Baker who, in the sixteenth century, had founded a school that was held in the tower of Holy Trinity Church. The two incomes, thus combined, supported a new school set up in the Cloth Hall which was known as the Archbishop Abbot's School. It closed in 1933. The present George Abbot Schools are a post-war foundation.

The tower still standing at the North Street end of the building is of mid-nineteenth-century vintage and was built for the school on part of the workhouse site. Oddly enough, the old workhouse was not entirely destroyed, as evidence of a roof line can still be seen on the tower, and part of the building remained until 1907 as a public house.

Another important building gained by the town in the seventeenth century was Child House. It was built by a Mayor of Guildford, John Child, and, like the Guildhall, it probably has a façade—also of wood—placed in front of earlier work.

Child House was purchased by the corporation in 1957 and its name changed to Guildford House. It underwent some restoration, and is now used as a centre for exhibitions, lectures, and meetings. It is a perfect example of the re-use of an old house and is a credit to the town.

Inside, the staircase is exceptionally good. Each newel is topped with a basket of fruit and flowers carved in wood, and terminated with a floral pendant. There are plaster ceilings in the first-floor room at the front, also in the rear ground floor, or garden, room. Both are most probably contemporary with the frontage, but not of the same quality as the stair.

Opposite Abbot's Hospital is Holy Trinity Church which was almost entirely rebuilt in 1751–63 by James Horne after the collapse of the tower of the medieval church. The only part of the old church remaining is the sixteenth-century Weston Chantry Chapel. Extensions at the east end were made by Sir Arthur Blomfield in 1888.

There are many memorials inside, but the tomb of George Abbot of 1635 is a fine example of its kind. It is the work of Matthias and John Christmas whose father, Gerard, was carver to the Navy. The Christmas workshops were in Cripplegate and the tomb was probably commissioned by George Abbot's brother, a City merchant, who would have known the Christmas family. Their work would have appealed to him, one might im-

*Guildford House has a front of about 1660. It is now the property of the town and is used for art exhibitions and lectures*

agine, since it was conservative and somewhat old-fashioned.

A school was founded in 1509 by Robert Beckingham on a site in Castle Street, and one of its governors was the prior of the Dominican Friary in Guildford. After the suppression of chantries the school was refounded under Royal Charter by Edward VI in 1553—the document is still preserved. This was Guildford's Royal Grammar School.

The building of the old school on the present site in the Upper High Street began in 1557 with the southern range opposite the entrance. Then followed the west wing with the masters' lodging in 1571 and, finally, the street frontage was built in 1586. It is in Bargate stone, probably intended to be whitewashed.

As the eighteenth century drew to a close, road improvements were being made in Surrey, encouraged by the growing need for easier communication between London, Portsmouth and Brighton. The better roads naturally created a demand for an increase in accommodation for travellers and horses alike. In 1830 some nineteen coaches a day were passing through Guildford, and as the town was one day's journey from both Portsmouth and London it was well placed for the inn trade.

As John Aubrey, the antiquary, noted in the seventeenth century, the town had always been famous for its good inns, and many of these remained until the present century. They included the Red Lion, below the Guildhall, where Evelyn, a diarist, stayed in 1664 and Pepys, a regular visitor when on Navy business, reported the asparagus as being "the best I have ever eat in my life". Timothy Whites now occupies the site.

The White Hart was pulled down to make way for a Sainsbury's shop in 1905—a shop that itself has been replaced by a larger store backed by a monstrous multi-storey car park. Woolworth's has taken the place of the White Lion, where Turner made a little sketch of Quarry Street from one of the upper windows.

Guildford still has the Angel Hotel which has an undercroft of the thirteenth century—it never had any religious purpose, but like a similar one across the road under No. 72, it was a shop beneath a merchant's house.

The steep, cobbled hill of the High Street provides a setting both unusual and flattering for the buildings of interest that survive and flank it. The shop-fronts are almost all modern and of the usual unlikeable kind, but above the shops there is a fair sprinkling of early frontages besides those of the larger buildings mentioned already. Guildford High Street is still undoubtedly one of the most impressive streets in the South-East.

There is a fine Baroque house at the bottom of the High Street, girdled around with a shop-front designed for the display of tailor's dummies. Nos. 43–45 High Street have nineteenth-century fronts.

*Guildford's Royal Grammar School, first founded in 1509 and refounded by Edward VI in 1553*

*The Corona Restaurant is one of the town's old houses and dates mostly to the seventeenth century. It is now known as Pizzaland*

A seventeenth-century building, once known as the Corona Restaurant, adds character to the north side of the High Street with its projecting bay. Unfortunately, the old tea-shop atmosphere of this place has gone. However, no external changes have been made so far.

There are several late eighteenth-century doorcases dotted along the High Street, and the pretty frontage of Lloyds Bank is worth looking at. There is a good late eighteenth-century doorcase at No. 242 in the upper part of the High Street and also, near the grammar school, one of the last remaining large town houses of the late seventeenth century, the brick-built Somerset House. It has a pedimented centre in the Dutch style which might possibly be a reconstruction.

Although there have been many changes in Quarry Street, part of it has remained unspoilt. This includes the home of the Guildford Museum and Muniment Room, Castle Arch and its early improvements made by Francis Carter when he moved there from the castle in 1630 and the much later additions designed by the architect, Ralph Nevill, F.S.A., who died in 1917. Two very good chalk fireplaces and some panelling remain in the house from the seventeenth century while the adjoining arch is part of the old castle, probably mid-thirteenth-century work.

Nearby is Castle House with a heavy, late eighteenth-century doorcase. On the opposite side of the road is Rosemary Alley which leads down to Millbrook from

*Caleb Lovejoy Almshouses, built in 'Tudor' style in 1838, now the best building of its kind in a town that is rapidly losing many buildings of character*

where the backs of the houses in Quarry Street can be seen on the cliff-like slope of the ground. The picturesque quality remains to some extent, but it is being changed by new work, some of which resembles an open chest of drawers.

On the other side of Millbrook in its setting amid trees on a tiny island can be seen the Yvonne Arnaud Theatre which stands apart, almost unseen, making no architectural impact on the town. The Town Mill, nearby, is a plain brick building and looks out of place, especially in relation to the nearby departmental store, an architectural disaster that should never have been built on this riverside site.

But to return to Quarry Street—on the steeply-rising ground above the southern end is Racks Close, now a public open space, its name recalls the days of the Guildford cloth trade when dyed cloth was hung there on racks to dry.

Many factors have contributed to the expansion and redevelopment of Guildford that began in the nineteenth century and is still taking place. Provision for the flow of traffic is now a regrettable cause of change, but perhaps the first and greatest single influence was the coming of the railway in 1845 that linked the town with the London terminal at Nine Elms. Further impetus came with the extension of the line to Portsmouth and the arrival of other lines, in particular the line from Surbiton to Guildford's London Road station in 1885.

Developments begun to the north of the town in the 1820s and 1830s along Stoke Road where, until this time, Parson's Almshouses, built in 1796, had stood in open fields with only Stoke Park mansion (destroyed in 1978) a few late framed houses in Josephs Road, and Stoke Church.

The Gothick style Stoke Hotel, with its cast-iron porch, was built by 1800 as a private house and, further along Stoke Road, Victoria Terrace with similar developments was begun in the 1850s. Other early nineteenth-century developments were along Portsmouth Road, west of the river, where there are several pairs of very elegant stuccoed villas in the classical style.

Along Epsom Road, and the area to the east, there was extensive development from the mid-nineteenth century, and a variety of villas and cottages were built in many styles exploiting a decorative use of flint, stone, brick and external woodwork—the latter particularly for bargeboards. The property of this period in the town is now equally important as the earlier work that survives.

The development of the Warwick's Bench area came also in the 1900s, and the house with most character is Durbins in Chantrey View Road, built by Roger Fry for himself around 1913. It is a severe house in a classical style and still has murals in the entrance hall by Vanessa Bell and Duncan Grant.

Towards the end of the nineteenth century some high quality building was done west of the river at Bury Fields.

*The great modern cathedral on Stag Hill, Guildford*

The pretty Tudor-style Caleb Lovejoy Almshouses were built in 1838 with money from properties at Southwark left by Caleb Lovejoy who died in 1676. These and Westbury House, a mid-seventeenth-century building with an eighteenth-century front, belong to an earlier period and survive together with St Nicolas's Church.

Of the later period, Thackeray Turner's Wycliffe Buildings (1894) exploit a difficult site with great success, his Mead Cottage (1895) is a delightful essay in the local vernacular style and The Court (1902) is a successful achievement in planning very advanced for its time. The massive bulk of the Central Electricity Generating Board's offices is the result of a series of bone-headed planning errors made in recent years.

Further west, along Portsmouth Road, is Norman Shaw's Rectory Place of 1880 with tile-hung gables typical of his style. In Guildown there are houses by Lutyens (Littlecroft, 1899) and Voysey (Littleholm, 1907).

Since the 1939–45 war Guildford has been surrounded by extensive developments spreading out towards Jacobs Well and Worplesdon to the north and Merrow to the east. Nearer the centre, the developments on and around Stag Hill have produced a housing estate, a badly designed university complex, and a cathedral.

Sir Edward Maufe's red-brick cathedral enjoys a good site—good for a lighthouse—but not for a cathedral, and the dull, pinched exterior does not survive the ordeal. The handling of the interior space, however, is exceptionally good and the minimal use of decoration—a necessity in these times—has enhanced the effect of light and space.

# CHAPTER THREE

# Nonsuch Park to Merrow

An area of countryside to the north of Ewell appealed to Henry VIII as a suitable extension to his hunting grounds centred upon Hampton Court. It was a convenient place for a small hunting lodge which, when combined with Oatlands, would enable the ageing king to continue his hunting without a long ride to and from Hampton Court.

The village of Cuddington stood where Henry wanted to build, and the lord of the manor, Richard Codington, was not foolish enough to deny the king's wishes. The parish church was already in the king's hands as it had been under the patronage of Merton Priory, then not long suppressed. So the manor of Cuddington was acquired in the summer of 1538, and in 1540 was annexed to the Honour of Hampton Court, a vast royal park extending from Middlesex to Surrey.

The building of Nonsuch began in 1538 and for the embellishments—the carving and plasterwork and many other refinements—foreign craftsmen were brought in to an extent never before seen in England.

Queen Mary had little interest in Nonsuch, but Elizabeth enjoyed the park for the hunting and she spent much time there until her death in 1603. James I and his queen also visited the palace, but it was beginning to be too old-fashioned for the Court. After the Restoration during the Plague and the Great Fire it was used as government offices, but then it passed to Barbara Villiers the mistress of Charles II. By 1682 demolition had begun, the proceeds from which she used to pay her debts.

The Tudor mansion stood in the Little Park, but in the Great Park a new building, Worcester House, had succeeded the old keeper's house. Keeper's Lodge, an old framed house, survived and became known as Worcester Park Farm.

It was at this farmhouse that the Pre-Raphaelites worked in the year 1851. Holman Hunt and John Millais had begun work earlier in that year based on lodgings at Kingston; Millais was painting *Ophelia* and Holman Hunt *The Hireling Shepherd*. After the move to the farm, they continued work on these pictures. Millais seems to have been working on his *Ophelia* somewhere along the little Hogsmill stream, but the garden of the old house also provided backgrounds for Millais's *The Huguenot* and Holman Hunt's *The Light of the World*.

At Ewell the junction of Church Street and the High Street was the ancient centre of the village, and until its demolition in 1800 a seventeenth-century market house stood there. Church Street was then the main road to London; the present road, out past the telephone exchange and the new church, was not cut until 1834.

Several of the houses in Ewell, although appearing to be brick built, are clad in mathematical tiles that look very convincingly like bricks. There is a good example of this in Church Street, near the old watch-house. A fragment of

*Princes Stand, Epsom Downs, built in 1897, a survival of the days when Parliament took the day off and M.P.s attended the Derby Day meeting*

a much older house remains in Fitznells, part of which has a fifteenth-century crownpost roof, although the exterior is so stuccoed that it might be entirely of the nineteenth century.

There is a row of continuous jetty cottages of about 1600 in the High Street that have been rendered in rough cast and have had some later sash-windows inserted. Well House in Church Street is a handsome house of the early eighteenth century: it retains its original sashes, but I suspect a later face-lift that introduced the double porch with Tuscan columns and the bow window. Later, but also very much in a vernacular style, are a few white weatherboarded houses in Well Street.

Bourne Hall once stood in the small park at the centre of the village until it was allowed to fall into decay, and then had to be pulled down in 1970. The house, built in the late eighteenth century, was a considerable ornament to Ewell, but now there is on the site a large circular building, rather like an alien spaceship, which houses the library, exhibition gallery and meeting rooms.

Unfortunately, Ewell also lost its old church when a new one was built to replace it in 1848. Only the old tower of flint and stone, part chequer-work, remains. Nearby is Ewell Castle, a large castellated house of about the time of Waterloo.

Epsom is associated with racing and probably few people today would now also connect it with the salts that bear its name. For a short period, from the mid-seventeenth century, the town prospered as a spa and the court of Charles II went there to take the waters.

During the early period of the spa, Church Street, from the High Street to the church, was a favourite parade. However, the church of those days has now gone with the exception of the tower.

The first re-build was in 1825 and was in the style of reedy Gothic known as Commissioners' Gothic. Then, in 1907, plans to enlarge the building were put in hand. This work resulted in the replacement of the east end and the transepts in a large-scale style that is spacious but characterless. In 1968 the temporary join between the 1825 work and that of 1907 was made permanent, and all intentions to complete the programme of enlargement were abandoned.

By the 1730s Epsom had begun a rapid decline as a spa. Before this it had gained some notable houses, in particular the New Inn—now Waterloo House—of about 1690. Other houses of the period are Woodcote Grove in Chalk Lane (1680); The Hylands and Hylands House in Dorking Road (early eighteenth century); and Ashley House in Ashley Road, now the Registrar's Office. Its date is 1769 and it has an Adam doorcase.

In Church Street there is a row opposite the church including The Cedars (early eighteenth century); Richmond House (probably a seventeenth-century house with

a nineteenth-century stuccoed front) and the old King's Head.

Opposite here was Pitt Place, one of the most interesting and important eighteenth-century houses in Epsom. It stood empty for a time, and regardless of two building preservation orders, it was quickly, almost secretly, demolished in 1967. Much detail in the house is thought to have come from Nonsuch, but all has now vanished.

At Woodcote Park there is the house built by the sixth Lord Baltimore and attributed to Isaac Ware, the early eighteenth-century architect of old Chesterfield House, London. It was damaged by fire in 1934 but has been restored. Near the entrance to the park is a round, brick pigeon-house and a seventeenth-century brick barn.

From Woodcote the lanes lead to Ashtead Park where the present house, built by Bonomi in 1790, is the third on the site. It is now a school.

Ashtead Church stands in the north-west corner of the park, and is notable for its sixteenth-century tower and the Horsham slab roofs of the nave and chancel. The whole church was restored with too much enthusiasm in 1862, an enthusiasm that ran to a riot of elaboration when it came to the timber roofs.

Ashtead almost imperceptibly merges into Leatherhead, joined by late nineteenth-century, and more recent housing developments. On the north-western approaches to the town this includes some building for light industry and

*Sweech House was restored in 1951 and is one of the finest timber-framed houses in Leatherhead. It has been much altered and added to, the centre portion may contain early sixteenth-century work but the two wings date to after 1600*

a depressing shabbiness that seems inevitably to be associated with such areas.

Leatherhead's most interesting buildings are around the old centre, above the River Mole. From the river bridge, and the nearby Running Horse, a few nineteenth-century houses line Bridge Street which ends, at the top of the hill, at the junction of the town's principal roads.

At this crossing there is a mock-Tudor bank and other less inspiring buildings, but there is also a pharmacy shop-front with fluted Doric columns and a pestle and mortar over the fascia. Then round the corner in North Street is another later nineteenth-century shop-front with a canopy supported by cast iron brackets.

Returning to the centre, Sweech House in Gravel Hill is a well-restored house and has now returned to one occupancy after being sub-divided since the early nineteenth century. The house appears to be of three builds or periods of growth, the centre section showing very slight evidence of being the oldest part and to this the crosswings were added after 1600.

In Church Street, No. 33 has a simple but charming early to mid-eighteenth-century brick front, but the building looks earlier at the back.

The Mansion, now council property, was built around 1740 but was revamped in the early nineteenth century—c.1830—with heavy portico, window architraves, and parapet. Beyond this is Wood Dene—called Wood

*No. 33 Church Street, Leatherhead, is older than it looks. It had a fashionable new brick front added in the mid-eighteenth century*

Villa when first built—a period piece of the mid-nineteenth century in an excessively opulent classical style.

Opposite Wood Dene is the parish church. The most unusual and striking feature about it is the large west tower, not only because it is sited above the main road on rising ground, but because it was set at a sharp angle by its fifteenth-century builders. This was done, it is said, because the churchyard boundary was very close and the only way room for processions round the outside of building could be made, was by angling the siting of the tower so that it encroached upon the south-west corner of the nave.

It is believed that the nave walls may, in part at least, be late Saxon and were pierced by the arcades in the thirteenth century. The arcade piers alternate in shape between circular and octagonal, and the capitals are all moulded, except one on the north side that has very fine trefoil foliage. The north and south transepts are *c.*1320 with a modern section added to the north to house the organ.

Beyond the bridge over the River Mole is Fetcham, now much built up. The exterior of the Old Rising Sun, now The Pilgrims Rest, has little to commend it, but inside there is part of a fifteenth-century hall with a crownpost roof.

The parish church of Fetcham is ancient and only modestly restored: the oldest parts are pre-Conquest, and the west wall of the nave and the wall above the south arcade with a deeply splayed window are early eleventh century.

Beyond Fetcham, the village street of Great Bookham runs at right angles between the upper and lower main roads. It still has some village character even after the changes that have taken place around it. The greatest loss in these developments was the Old Vicarage in the early 1960s—it had a very fine Adam-style entrance with portico.

The church dominates the scene with its ancient flint tower surmounted by a lovely weather-boarded upper stage and shingled spire. The south arcade of the nave is about 1150 and the north arcade a little later, the work

*St Mary's Church, Fetcham, is one of Surrey's oldest churches, the oldest parts are pre-Conquest and the lower parts of the tower are Norman*

*Polesden Lacey is set in some of the finest parkland in Surrey and the open-air theatre in the grounds
has become well known for its productions*

being similar to that at Fetcham.

Although there has been much recent housing development at Little Bookham, some corners of the old village remain. There is a fine range of barns at Maddox Farm, and there are more barns, in particular the so-called Tithe Barn, near the church. All are no earlier than 1600.

The church is probably twelfth century in origin and is under a single roof with an added bell-turret and modern porch. There was once a south aisle, and the blocked south arcade is similar to the one at Great Bookham.

In 1630 Anthony Rous bought the estate of Polesden Lacey, a mile or two away, and built a house there which was subsequently owned by the dramatist Richard Brinsley Sheridan. Two years after his death his son sold the house in 1818 for £10,000 to Joseph Bonsor who demolished it and employed Thomas Cubitt, then at the beginning of his career, to build another, a pleasant villa typical of the post-Napoleonic War period.

After the death of Bonsor, the house was owned in turn by Sir Walter Farquhar, Bt., Sir Clinton Dawkins, and Captain the Honourable Ronald Henry Fulke Greville who died in 1908, and whose widow continued to live there until her death in 1942.

The house and estate of a thousand acres were left to the National Trust by Mrs Greville as a memorial to her father, the Right Honourable William McEwan, P.C. It is one of the most attractive of the houses in the county open to the public.

West of Little Bookham is the village of Effingham, the centre of which is near the church and around The Street where there are several houses of interest. Browns, which was formerly the Manor House, is said to have "a very fine Tudor roof and two good Tudor brick chimneys" The house was faced in brick in the eighteenth century.

Old Westmore Cottage in Oreston Lane, just off The Street, has a large porch in the 1630–50 decorative brick style placed in front of a framed cottage that may be the building mentioned in the Byfleet Court Rolls of 1496 and 1547.

The parish church has suffered very heavy restoration, although the crownpost roof in the south transept may be fifteenth century.

Norwood Farm is a large hall house of the fifteenth century and has many high quality features including a moulded centre-of-hall crownpost and an easily identifiable cross passage with doors to the buttery and pantry.

Mention must be made of the Corpus Domini convent. Part of it has been identified as the Red House designed by Sir Edwin Lutyens in 1893 for Susan Muir-Mackenzie. It is in red brick with stone dressings and reflects some of Lutyens's style, but the house does not appear to warrant the claim made by some writers that it was one of his important early houses. However, there have been alterations and additions, and these could have changed its

*The garden front of Horsley Towers, built by Sir Charles Barry 1820–9, and added to in a highly personal and eccentric style by Lord Lovelace in the 1850s*

*Lord Lovelace built many houses in the village of East Horsley and The Manor House is typical of his very individual style*

original character quite considerably.

William King, eldest son of Peter, seventh Lord King, Baron of Ockham, was born in 1805 and at the age of twenty-eight he inherited the title. In 1835 he married Augusta Ada, the only legitimate daughter of the poet, Lord Byron, and this marriage has led to much misunderstanding about Byron's connection with Horsley, in fact Byron never owned property there, much less lived in the village.

William, Lord King, created Earl of Lovelace in 1838, purchased from a Mr Currie in 1840 what was then known as East Horsley House. By 1846 he had decided to move from Ockham Park and make East Horsley House, later to become known as Horsley Towers, his principal seat.

This house at East Horsley was built in the 1820s by Barry, architect of the Houses of Parliament, in a plain Tudor style, and to this house Lord Lovelace began to make additions. In 1847 he built a large banqueting hall, and his ability as an innovator is shown here in the roof where timbers that had been bent by steam heat were used for the arched trusses.

Lord Lovelace's wife, Augusta Ada, died in 1852, and after a while abroad he returned to East Horsley and began the unusual architectural work in polychrome brick with which his name is associated. In 1858–9 he built on to the Towers the large 'Rhenish' tower by the lake, the cloisters, and the remarkable tunnel approach to the

*The Old Cottage, West Horsley, is typical of several medieval houses in the village, but has an unusual chamfered crownpost in its roof*

*St Mary's Church, West Horsley, has happily escaped drastic restoration, the unbuttressed flint tower is probably early work*

house. In the 1860s he began building cottages, lodges, and bridges in the village and on the estate.

West Horsley and East and West Clandon are particularly interesting villages. At West Horsley the cottage, Sumners, is probably of very early date, around 1350. It had a large two-bay open hall, and has an unusually large sans-purlin roof—no longitudinal bracing except that provided by the cladding. Of many other important houses, two that should not go unnoticed are the Old Cottage and Winterfold which stand almost side by side and are both fifteenth-century hall houses. They each have crownpost roofs, and Winterfold has a good mid-seventeenth-century crosswing.

West Horsley Place is a large house with sections dating at least to the fifteenth century, but with many sixteenth-century and later additions and changes. The brick front, which is similar to Slyfield, near Leatherhead, in style, dates to about 1630 and was probably built for the second Lord Montague. More work on the front was done about 1749 by Henry Weston. This probably included the shortening of the east wing and insertion of windows, and the parapet and over-large central gable with lunette window may also date to this time. The dog kennels flanking each side of the front are an attractive feature.

West Horsley Church is not in the village, but at the side of the main road. It has, fortunately, been spared any drastic restoration and remains essentially thirteenth century. The tower may be older as it has no buttresses and is arranged in three recessed stages. It is capped with a late fourteenth-century shingled broach spire. The west porch is also said to be late fourteenth century, but I think this is unlikely. The roof reconstruction is with kingposts and ridge-piece, an almost unknown traditional form for Surrey and probably a late rebuild. It is claimed that the head of Sir Walter Ralegh is buried in St Nicholas Chapel, interred there by his son, Carew, in 1660.

There is a possibility that a large house once stood to the south-west of the church on a mound at the rear of Church House. Whether Church House could have been any part of the layout of this house, or a building serving some purpose in relation to the church, has yet to be discovered. However, it is certain that its timber-frame structure is very uncommon, and suggests that it did not have the usual domestic use. The house has jetties at the front and back, and is under a good crownpost roof of, perhaps, about 1500.

At East Clandon are the entrance gates to Hatchlands, a red-brick Palladian-style house built, and probably designed, by Admiral Boscawen in 1756–7. The interior decoration was by Robert Adam, and was executed at the start of his career in 1759.

In the village the little church of St Thomas gently dominates the scene. Church and cottages are small in scale and nothing seems out of place. If I had to single out one house as the most interesting it would be the late sixteenth-century Tunmore Cottage with its well-preserved framing and ogee braces.

In contrast, the larger West Clandon Church is not, in itself, very attractive, but with its tower of 1879 composes well with the small flint and timber-framed cottages opposite.

More West Clandon cottages are strung out along the road to Burnt Common and end at Dedeswell Manor, a hall house with a crosswing that was refronted in brick in the eighteenth century.

Plans for a new house at Clandon Park, the former seat of the Onslow family, are said to have been discussed as early as 1713 and the present house, designed by the Italian architect, Giacomo Leoni, was completed by about 1733.

The exterior is unremarkable, but the 1876 restorations may have been responsible for changes of a kind that have

*Tunmore Cottage at East Clandon is a charming example of later sixteenth-century timber-framing and has many well preserved original features*

*The much restored church of St Peter and St Paul, West Clandon, still has a few original features, the chancel roof may be fourteenth-century and the south porch fifteenth-century. The wooden spire was rebuilt in 1913 after a fire*

destroyed the subtleties of the original Palladian design.

Clandon Park, however, is famous for its interiors which have been so beautifully restored in recent years by the National Trust. The great Marble Hall with its strict Palladian proportions—it is a perfect cube —and delicately graduated tones of white and pale grey, together with the extraordinary 'marbled' columns, is unforgettable and provides the perfect introduction to a series of further rooms.

The Gubbay Collection of furniture, porcelain and needlework is also displayed in the house along with the Onslow family's pictures and furniture. The basement rooms have recently been converted into a military museum.

There is much residential redevelopment taking place at Merrow, and this will inevitably result in massive changes that will destroy its village character. The immediate benefit of the road changes has been to take the main road away from the church and to the north of the Old Farm-house.

Merrow Church, although attractive, is an almost complete rebuild of 1843–5, with a north aisle addition of 1881. The north porch door appears to be an original, moved and re-erected when the aisle was built.

The area to the east of the church, now the car park, was once the farmyard of the Old Farmhouse opposite, a large house of the mid- to late seventeenth century. The original main entrance was at the centre of the front, but has now been bricked up. This doorway led into a small lobby from which the original stair leads, and in which, on either side, are doors into the two front rooms. One of these rooms still contains a panelled dado and one remaining carved bracket that was used to fasten back an internal shutter. This room may have been the parlour.

*Clandon Park, the Palladian house built by Giacomo Leoni for Thomas Onslow and completed about 1739*

*The Marble Hall at Clandon is possibly the finest Palladian room in England. The plasterwork is believed to have been by Artari, and the fireplaces are by Rysbrack*

The larger of the two rear rooms was undoubtedly the kitchen, and it is believed to have a well near the centre of the floor. Upstairs there is much re-used high quality panelling.

Merrow has several other interesting houses, in particular Levylsdene (seventeenth to eighteenth century) which has a very good early seventeenth-century staircase. Merrow House (a plain brick house of 1802 and later but with some original detail), and the Horse and Groom. This last is a perfect example of its type and period—around 1650, I believe, regardless of the date 1615 painted on the front.

The woodwork throughout the house is very fine: most of the windows appear to be original, while many of the door frames have beautiful mouldings and carved chamfer stops typical of the period.

*The small Hunting Room, so-called after the tapestries with which it is hung, contains many porcelain pieces from the Gubbay Collection*

*Shalford Mill, now owned by the National Trust, may be visited by the public, and contains much of the original machinery*

# CHAPTER FOUR

# Shalford-Albury

The main road south-east out of Guildford used to be along Quarry Street, and then out towards Shalford where a small humpback bridge takes the road over the Tillingbourne stream.

Many mills have been powered by this small stream, one of which, Shalford Mill, still remains at the end of a narrow lane, opposite and a little to the south of the church. In 1932 it was sold for demolition, but fortunately was saved by the efforts of the Ferguson Gang and Godwin Austen, restored, and given to the National Trust.

The large, overhanging extension at the front is carried on large posts and contained the hoist. The structure is timber-framed, six bays long, and tile-hung above. The rear is weather-boarded from the second floor upwards with a lean-to carried over the stream on three arches—this is a little feature that must have attracted Ernest Shepard who used it for a drawing in *Now We Are Six*.

Near the mill is the old mill house, now known as The Old House. It is of several periods but the rear elevation is particularly interesting. It is in the decorative brick style of the 1650s and is contemporary with the mill.

Inside the house is a handsome stair with rusticated newel posts and pierced baluster panels—it is very like one at Slyfield Manor, near Leatherhead, another, larger house in the decorative brick style.

At Shalford are rows of what are probably seventeenth-century cottages, punctuated by one or two late eighteenth-century villas, around the Benjamin Ferrey Gothic-style parish church of 1846. The church is uninspired and replaces a classical building from which there are one or two monuments, notably those of the Austen family—one of 1759 by James Moorhouse and another of 1797 by Bacon.

Once hidden behind the church was Shalford Park mansion, home of the Austen family. The house was of great interest, not least the front entrance porch with Ionic columns that stood before an Adamesque door. All has gone, really as a result of public apathy in the face of the demands of the water authority which wanted the site.

Beyond the church and the surrounding cottages, the present main road leads past a pretty, framed cottage which had the *cottage orné* treatment in the nineteenth century and has ogee windows and large barge-boards. Then come Woodyer's very good school buildings of 1866–83, and next, over the railway bridge, a large open space where there are several nineteenth-century cottages, in particular Fosters Row of 1833 which is quite delightful.

The road eastwards leads to Chilworth, but since it forks past Great Tangley Manor to Wonersh and Shamley Green, a detour could be made to include these villages.

Architecturally, Great Tangley Manor is one of the more important houses in Surrey. In its original form it was an open hall house, but it is now important because in 1582 it was fronted with one of the finest examples of decorative timber framing in the county. The date is on one of the corbels. Later additions, notably the long covered way to the front entrance, were made by Philip Webb in 1886.

Beyond Great Tangley is Wonersh, a pleasant village centred around the Grantley Arms, a framed house that has undergone many changes in the pattern of its framing although the greater part of the original seventeenth-century build survives.

The small round shelter in the middle of the road opposite the Grantley Arms was constructed out of the old ice-house that once served the mansion of the Grantleys in Wonersh Park.

The village street is lined by several ancient houses, and one of these is The Cottage. It is of two builds side by side; the one is late work but the other is a fifteenth-century crosswing, small, but of superb workmanship, with a lavish use of large timbers. It is all that remains of a hall house and served as a very ostentatious parlour with an upper floor.

Opposite The Cottage are some framed houses that have undergone much restoration, and further along the street, towards Bramley, is a Wealden house so restored that it is now quite unrecognizable. Continuing in this direction one comes to the site of Wonersh Park mansion (demolished in 1935) and a brick gateway to the park through which one can take the short field path to the church.

Wonersh Church is a hotchpotch of medieval work with eighteenth-century rebuilding which was, in turn, partly remodelled by Sir Charles Nicholson when he rebuilt the east end in 1901.

The road to Shamley Green from Wonersh passes the Dower House, a handsome building said to be early eighteenth century, with a late doorcase of about 1790.

On the approach to Shamley Green, at a small cross-roads, is Lee Crouch, a fine example of a typical medieval hall house, the original build dating to the early fourteenth century.

At Lee Crouch the buttery and pantry at the service end can be identified by the mortice holes that once held the partition between them. Here also the upper service room is jettied out over the position of the cross passage which is a fairly unusual feature. The original parlour end was

The *Grantley Arms* is a late continuous jetty house. The framing of the walls has undergone changes and some of the ogee braces may be modern insertions

*The Dower House at Wonersh is a delightful example of eighteenth-century brickwork*

remodelled, probably in the sixteenth century when a first floor was inserted in the open hall. A further addition was made in the eighteenth century, but the original roof remains.

It is a superb crownpost construction revealing the smoke-covered timbers of the open hall section, the later insertion of a smoke bay when the hall was first floored, and the subsequent insertion of a brick chimney-stack. Most interesting of all is a deflector of lath and plaster so placed in the roof that it deflected the smoke from the open hearth in the hall below out through the small gablet above the hipped roof at the parlour end.

Between Lee Crouch and the green itself there are several cottages of somewhat later date. Watts Cottage, which is particularly handsome, was not a hall house, but was built around a brick stack from the outset. This cottage, and others adjoining it, indicate a possible old line for the road, which if extended would have taken it across the back garden of Lee Crouch.

The green at Shamley Green is quite extensive. Cutting across it is the road to Cranleigh, the lane to Farley Heath, and another back to Lordshill to join the road to Wonersh. There are many good houses of varying dates and styles surrounding it, and one or two houses are particularly fine.

The most prominent of these is The Malthouse with, behind it, Mellow House. This forms a complex group, and the framed structure with ogee braces and a jettied gable with original barge-boards is late Elizabethan. No other section abutting to it appears to be earlier, but Mellow House, some fourteen feet to the rear of it and a quite separate structure of good quality workmanship, is roughly contemporary.

In the corner of the green is Barn Cottage, once the post office, which is a fragment of a larger house and includes part of the old hall and a crosswing with a centre truss crownpost, now hidden in the roof space above a ceiling. The end of the house has disappeared—the remains of a fireplace can be seen high up in the gable end.

At the rear, only a foot or so away, there is a separate structure that could have been a detached kitchen that served the house when it was much larger.

South of the green, a short distance along the road to Cranleigh, are two houses sharing the odd name of Plunks.

Plunks Farm was a large hall house and retains the centre truss of the old hall complete with crownpost. It is interesting that this crownpost is virtually identical to the one in Barn Cottage. Both have an octagonal shaft with moulded capital and base, and both have four rising struts, two to the collar and two to the purlin.

Plunks Manor is of two distinct builds. One part is an old hall house with crownpost roof. The other part, a crosswing, is of particularly high quality work and the

*Watts Cottage at Shamley Green is a typical small Surrey cottage of the late sixteenth century and its position may indicate the earlier line of the road*

carved barge-boards—which must be original—are only equalled by those at the rear of Nursecombe Farm, Bramley, or those on a smaller scale on The Malthouse, only two or three hundred yards away.

To the west of the green, a lane loops at the back of the village to Lordshill and meets the road to Wonersh, near Lee Crouch. There are several good houses along this lane.

Hullhatch has a crosswing of the later fifteenth-century,

65

*Barnett Farm was built about 1600 with the ceilings of the first-floor rooms constructed below the eaves level to give more headroom in the roof space where servants and farm-workers slept*

the only part surviving of an early hall house that has otherwise quite gone.

Further along the lane is Yieldhurst. This house also has its origins in the fifteenth century and was a hall house. Much of the old hall remains—soot can be seen on the roof timbers—although floors and ceilings have been inserted. The large crosswing is later than the one at Hull-

hatch—it may well be *c.*1600—and it replaces the parlour end of the original hall house. The long, lapping braces in the walls of the old hall that pass from wallplate to sill are an indication of early work although the roof appears to be of the side purlin type and probably not earlier than 1500.

In the fields behind Yieldhurst is Barnett Farm, a complete house of about 1600. It was built as a farmhouse with a large chimney-stack on the side providing for a wide, open kitchen fireplace (now blocked) at which all the cooking was done. The same stack also served another fireplace on the upper floor where it heated the best parlour.

Accommodation for servants and farmworkers was provided in the roof space where added headroom was made by the introduction of a second 'wallplate' so that the first-floor ceilings were constructed some two feet below the tiebeams and the true wallplates.

After this slight digression, the route eastward is taken up again at Chilworth in the beautiful Tillingbourne Valley. The stream was here harnessed for the production of gunpowder and paper. William Cobbett reported that the paper was used for bank notes—he was probably wrong in this assertion—and in his *Rural Rides* he condemned the combination as particularly evil. Now all this activity has ceased.

We read of mills at Chilworth, owned by Sir Edward

Randyll, being leased in the 1630s to the East India Company. By 1636 the Chilworth mill-owners were the only manufacturers in the country authorized by the Crown, but the monopoly was not complete and much illicit manufacture continued. In 1641 the royal monopoly ceased by an Act of Charles I.

The Chilworth mills were in production during the Civil War and provided powder for the Parliamentarian forces. After the Restoration they continued, and the name of Vincent Randyll is found in contracts of the 1670s. In his *Natural History and Antiquities of the County of Surrey* Aubrey gives Morgan Randyll as the owner of the mills "in this little romancy vale". Mills at Albury are also recorded while at Shere a mill blew up and flying debris knocked off the head of a woman as she sat spinning in her cottage!

The mills continued in production throughout the nineteenth century, and in the 1800s they were greatly enlarged. In the 1914–18 war they played an important part in the supply of munitions, but have now been abandoned.

Chilworth Manor house was the home of some of the owners of the mills in the valley below. The site of the present mansion has a tenuous connection with a cell of the Austin Canons who administered the chapel of St Martha and the lake in the gardens is claimed to have been a stewpond.

As a result of the many changes of owners and their fortunes, Chilworth Manor house is a complicated mixture of styles. Early work may be represented by the present front wing which is in the decorative brick style of the seventeenth century, but which is suspect in that, at the very least, it has been heavily restored. The formal garden, said by some to be late seventeenth century and by others to have been built for the Duchess of Marlborough around 1730, is surrounded by a restored brick wall in the seventeenth-century style of the front. Regardless of when or for whom it was built, this terraced garden on the hillside is a heavenly place.

Above Chilworth and the modern roadways, an ancient route comes across the Downs from Shalford, after crossing the Wey at St Catherine's, and reaches the church of St Martha.

The earliest work that has been identified at St Martha's Chapel dates to 1190, and it was about this time that the church was granted to the priory of St Thomas the Martyr at Aldebury (Newark at Ripley). Although granted to Newark, the dedication to St Martha remained until 1464 when it became St Martha and All Holy Martyrs.

Despite the fact that the idea of great numbers of pilgrims using the route across the Downs has been discredited, the notion of the chapel being used as a kind of stop-over for a few pilgrims cannot be dismissed. Financial benefit for Newark Priory from this source seems likely

*Chilworth Manor is beautifully sited on the slopes of the Downs and in the past was the home of some of the owners of the gunpowder mills in the valley below*

from existing records, and there is a record, dated 1463, of an indulgence granted to pilgrims to—or benefactors of—the church of St Martha and All Holy Martyrs.

Beyond St Martha's, the so-called Pilgrims' Way crosses Albury Downs. To the south is the present Albury village—once known as Weston Street before the original village was removed from Albury Park. Newlands Corner is on the high ground to the north.

There are few more pleasant places than Newlands Corner on a warm summer evening, for although there may be many people near the car park, most will have gone there to do nothing more energetic than stare at the distant view or stroll over the grassy slopes. Or to wait for the sun to set and listen, as the last blackbird ceases his evening song, to the lingering solitary song of the nightingale as he trills through his repertoire in the thick, low bushes.

Although the views from Newlands Corner are no less extensive than those from the Hog's Back, the landscape is more intimate: a division of tiny fields between solid banks of dark woodland and groups of houses and farms tenderly held in the hollows of the gentle hills give a jewel-like quality to the landscape.

One is constantly tempted to look at the detail—at a man and girl walking a field path a mile away across the valley, at the curl of smoke from a gardener's bonfire, or to be fascinated by the way the deep emerald shadows of

the grazing cattle streak the golden-green turf.

Below Newlands Corner the old Albury village, now vanished, and the church formed a settlement dating back at least to Saxon times when the place was called Eldeberie. After the Conquest it was granted to Richard de Tonbridge who, in turn, rented it to Richard d'Abernon whose descendants continued to live there until the seventeenth century.

An engraving by Hollar of 1645 shows the old timber-framed mansion in Albury Park. This was largely rebuilt by John and George Evelyn for the Duke of Norfolk in the seventeenth century when they also laid out the gardens. The house was altered again in 1700, and yet again about 1800 by John Soane. More alterations were made by E.C. Hakewill and then Augustus Welby Pugin remodelled it almost entirely in 1846–52. The owner was then Henry Drummond, the banker, who earlier had Wilkins build him the Grecian 'Grange' in Hampshire.

Pugin did other work for Drummond including various houses in the 'new' Albury village, and he may have had a hand in the row with tall ornamental chimney-stacks often mistaken for authentic Tudor cottages.

From the eighteenth century, successive owners of Albury Park began a process of removing the old village, erecting fences, and diverting roads. Henry Drummond came at the end of the line and completed the process. Until the park was fenced and the village finally removed,

*Cookes Place, Albury, is a house of many periods, to the left is an
early crosswing with crownpost roof, and on the right is one of the
finest early seventeenth-century crosswings in the county*

the road from Newlands Corner came past the Silent Pool
towards the Apostolic Church, alongside Cookes Place, in
front of the Little George, once a public house (now a private dwelling), and out past the mansion to Shere.

The church was built by Pugin and William McIntosh
Brookes about 1840 for Mr Drummond who was a sup-
porter of Edward Irving, founder of the Catholic Apostolic Church.

Cookes Place, on the other hand, is old. It was added to

in the nineteenth century but much lovely original work
remains. A hall house with a crownpost roof can be identified, and there is an early crosswing at one end—also
with a crownpost roof—while at the other there is
another very fine later crosswing of the sixteenth or early
seventeenth century.

In the park, the medieval church of St Peter and St Paul
stands in front of what was once the village green.
Beyond, along the banks of the Tillingbourne, were the
village cottages, a few of which remained long enough to
be recorded on the 1839 Tithe Map. The sole survivor is
the timber-framed cottage across the stream, once the Little
George and home of the bailiff in Mr Drummond's time.

During the 1920s, the architect P.M. Johnson carried
out restoration work on the old church and wrote a long
report on its condition and age. He asserted that there was
a Saxon church on the site and that he found evidence of it
in the present building.

Inside the tower is a consecration cross which could
have been marked there by a Saxon bishop. But the tower
is most notable for its Norman work, especially the windows on the north side. The parapet is probably of the
same date as the cupola, which replaces an earlier spire,
and is of about 1750.

At the end of the thirteenth century a chancel—now
roofless—and a south transept were built. The nave was
probably re-roofed when the south aisle was added in the

fourteenth century and the arcade of three bays with columns standing on Sussex marble bases—really re-used capitals similar to the capitals in Ockham Church—are also of this date. I was shocked to see that these have recently been whitewashed.

The north porch was added in the fifteenth century. The barge-boards are original with beautifully carved quatrefoils, and it is interesting to see how this old design was copied by Victorian carvers of barge-boards elsewhere in the village.

The old church was closed for regular services in 1842, but not without a heated conflict between Martin Tupper, a great local eccentric who lived at Albury House, and Mr Drummond. Tupper got up a petition to try to keep the church open; but he failed and, most bitter rub of all, he was buried, not in the old graveyard, but up at the new church, built for the village by Mr Drummond in bright salmon-red brick. I have tried to like the new church, but I share Martin Tupper's sentiments.

Fortunately, the people of Albury have cared for their old church and worked hard to negotiate the best possible future for it. The church was declared redundant, and has been repaired. It is now safe and can fulfil a new role, that of merely existing as a thing of beauty.

*The old church of St Peter and St Paul, Albury, saved from decay by the determined efforts of villagers, and now as a redundant church, will be maintained for all time*

71

*The tower and spire of Shere church showing Lutyens's lych-gate, and a Wealden house to the right*

# CHAPTER FIVE

# Shere-Dorking-Buckland

Mercifully the A25 now bypasses Shere, a village with signs of ancient wealth if the considerable concentration of framed houses is to be taken into account. Numerous explanations have been offered for the obvious prosperity of the place from the fourteenth to the sixteenth centuries, but the Tillingbourne stream that flows through the village provided power for many activities along its banks, and it is likely that at Shere cloth manufacture was at least partly responsible for this prosperity.

The church has a large, shingled, thirteenth-century broach spire—not an elegant needle, but fat, comfortable and rustic, like a candle snuffer as it sits on the Norman tower. Transitional work of the late twelfth century always has a particular charm, and at Shere the emergence of new ideas can be seen in the clustered columns and capitals of Petworth marble in the arch between the south chapel and the south aisle. Of this period also is the west door into the nave.

In the north wall of the church there is a squint and a quatrefoil opening that belonged to a fourteenth-century anchorite cell. From documentary evidence published by the church, it appears that a young anchoress named Christine Carpenter was walled up in a cell attached to the church. Permission for this to be done—at the girl's own request—was given by the Bishop of Winchester in 1329, after a full examination of her by the rector and parishioners. It seems that Christine then came out of her cell, for by 1332 another application was made for her return for fear of excommunication.

One cannot help wondering what pressures were brought to bear upon this poor creature, deluded to submit to being walled up and perpetually confined.

Space prevents a description of all the many interesting houses in the village, but two or three must be mentioned, in particular Vine Cottages. Once a large single farmhouse known as Rolls, they are the result of growth and change from a hall house of about 1450. Crosswings have been added—the jettied one to the east is of about 1500 and the western crosswing is mid-seventeenth century. The buildings at the rear of the western crosswing may once have been a detached kitchen.

In the square is a lych-gate by Lutyens, and a house on the south side that is probably a Wealden type. Part is now called Rookery Nook (no need to wonder when this name first appeared)! Another Wealden-type house that is much more easily recognized is in Lower Street.

Quite a number of nineteenth-century houses line Middle Street—the main street—but they blend well with the old houses that include Forge Cottage and Bodryn, a fifteenth-century hall house with a seventeenth-century crosswing. The group of properties including the post office is a complicated development ranging from early fifteenth century at the southern end to seventeenth century at the other.

Like Shere, Gomshall is on the Tillingbourne—it still has a mill, admittedly modified for use as a restaurant and no longer working. Across the stream, over a humpback bridge, is the Gomshall Tannery on the site of a tan-yard, the last survivor of many that flourished in this valley, dating back at least to the sixteenth century.

On rising ground to the north of the main road, opposite the tannery shop, is a barn which is probably late sixteenth century and belongs to Edmonds farmhouse. The barn is hipped at both ends and has a large roof. The farmhouse, down near the main road, is mid-fifteenth century and was built as a hall house.

At the corner of the main road and Queen Street is a house once known as Tannery House, later as Ivy House, and now as King John House. There was a tannery there at least as early as the sixteenth century and part of an early fifteenth-century house remains at the rear of the present building which is one of the really good brick houses of its

period in the district.

Along Queen Street is a framed house, Nos. 9–12, probably sixteenth century, and built as a farmhouse. In the eighteenth century a third tannery was started there, but it had closed down by the end of the century. At the crossroads, further on, is Monks House which was reputedly built by a blacksmith in the mid-seventeenth century.

Westwards near the railway are Malthouse Cottages, and then, beyond the railway bridge, is Tower Hill Manor. Malthouse Cottages, originally a farmhouse with farmyard and barns which were taken away when the railway was built, is the result of three periods of building. The centre section was a hall house and the crosswing with decorative framing was added in the early seventeenth century. The curved braces in this wing are reminiscent of work at Bramley Manor and Great Tangley. The other crosswing is of a late date—it could be identified as eighteenth century.

Cloth was made at Shere, leather at Gomshall, and at Abinger Hammer the Tillingbourne was harnessed to give power for an iron-mill. It is difficult to imagine that this now peaceful place was once a centre of industry.

The road enters Abinger Hammer past Old Hatch Farm, the oldest part of which was standing in the fifteenth century and had a crosswing added to it during the time of the iron-mills in the sixteenth century.

After narrowing at a double turn round the pub, the

*King John House, one of the best small Jacobean brick houses in the district was built about 1620.*
*Part of a much earlier framed house remains at the rear*

*Malthouse Cottages were described as "a house with a malthouse" in 1843, but the first reference to a malthouse was in 1677*

roadway opens into a kind of square formed by the pub's private car park. Here is Clock House which, although it dates only to the 1900s, is tile-hung in the traditional Surrey way. Past Clock House is a wide green and across this a lane runs to Sutton, Holmbury St Mary and Forest Green.

At Sutton is Fulvens Farm, a brick house of the mid-seventeenth century with a long, two-storey front, projecting two-storeyed gabled porch, and panelled work in the brick chimney-stacks. The best of its kind in the county.

The area south of Abinger Hammer is remote even now. It is an area of woods and heath on a sandstone belt crossing the county south of the chalk. Ways across from north to south were never easy, and along the old tracks, now surfaced, the sandstone banks rise sheer for twenty—sometimes thirty—feet and trees meet overhead.

At Friday Street with its woodland lake, once a mill-pond, the colours are good at all times of the year, but in autumn the sun might catch the russet brown of the trunks of some large trees at the water's edge, and then there is colour indeed.

South of Friday Street is Leith Hill with its famous tower at the highest point in Surrey. The tower was built in 1766 for Richard Hull who, it is said, requested to be buried beneath it. It was restored—or remodelled—by W. Evelyn in 1864 and given a stair turret, and an upper platform to raise the height to exactly 1,000 feet above sea level.

Holmbury St Mary is a pretty village, and without intending to be derogatory, one feels this is what the Victorians set out to make it. Besides the cottages there are many nineteenth-century mansions, in particular the house that W.E. Street built for himself, and there is also the church he built at his own expense in 1879.

Abinger Church was badly damaged by a bomb in 1944, and then, after restoration, the tower and roof were again hit—by lightning. Little original detail has, therefore, survived and the church is now an example—a creditable one—of what modern restoration, combined with even more reconstruction, can achieve. Here at least some lessons have been learnt from the errors of the nineteenth century.

Outside the church are the village stocks, and the village pound is still in the garden of Abinger Manor Cottage.

Abinger Manor is a much altered house with a little sixteenth-or seventeenth-century brickwork in the porch. However, in the garden there is a Norman motte or mound upon which a wooden, fortified structure was placed. The post holes of this building have been found and are marked. At the back of Abinger Manor are the scanty remains of a Mesolithic pit dwelling.

Opposite the church is Abinger Hatch of which William Bray, the historian, recorded in his diary: 'July 23

*Crossways Farmhouse, Abinger, is one of the finest examples of mid-seventeenth-century decorative brickwork in the county. Galleted Bargate stonework and a Horsham tile roof combine with the brick and add to the great charm of this house*

1759. To the Hatch to dinner'. He concludes, '. . . left at 7; paid for dinner and wine, 4s. 6d.'

A short distance to the south is St James's Well with a well-head of 1893 and an inscription in Greek indicating that the water is of the best. Goddards, opposite, is one of Lutyens's larger houses and was built in 1899.

Returning to the A25, and at the corner of the main road and the lane down towards Holmbury St Mary is Crossways Farm. It stands behind a high wall and alongside a farmyard and barns. The whole group is quite perfect, in particular the farmhouse which is an example of early to mid-seventeenth-century brickwork of the kind used elsewhere in Surrey at Shalford House and in Godalming High Street. The free interpretation of classical mouldings in brick is here done more confidently than is usual, also the decoration has been used with restraint and is, therefore, more effective. Honey-coloured Bargate sandstone galleted with ironstone combines with the deep earth red of the bricks, and the mortar looks as delectable as farmhouse cream.

Wotton, long associated with the Evelyn family, is a mile away from Crossways Farm. This is another place where everything combines to produce a kind of completeness, but here it might be imagined to be as much by natural forces as by man's design.

The church has been restored, but the tower has been little harmed, and from the road it is this that one sees

*Wotton Church, beautifully sited on an ancient religious site in the gentle folds of the North Downs*

across the valley, for trees discreetly veil the nave and chancel.

It is possible that the tower is by far the oldest part of the church, and it is probably Saxon work in parts. Excavation has revealed foundations west of the tower that could be earlier than 1050, and the fact that the tower is widest from north to south could be because it was built on the walls of an early chancel. It was in this tower that young John Evelyn, the diarist, attended school.

In the Evelyn Chapel, on the north side of the present chancel, are some very good alabaster memorials—one to George Evelyn, purchaser of Wotton, who died in 1603, and another to Richard Evelyn, father of the famous John. The tombs of John and his wife are plain and coffin-shaped with white marble tops carrying inscriptions.

The rambling brick house that George Evelyn bought in 1579 has been changed so many times that little of the older work can be seen. Kent contributed the orangery, Hawksmoor the old library in the eighteenth century, and in 1864 Woodyer did some work there in the Tudor style, including the Gothic library.

The gardens, largely landscaped by John Evelyn and for which Wotton was famous, have survived in part.

Past Wotton the road dips steeply downwards between high sandstone banks to Westcott where there is a well-sited small church built by Sir George Gilbert Scott in 1852 on a hill above the road to the south-west of the village. The group of houses including The Barracks has Horsham slab roofs and some decorative seventeenth-century brickwork—a very good example of a combination of stone and brick.

East of Westcott is Milton Street, a lane that ends at the entrance to Old Bury Hill lake, now run commercially as a fishing lake, and Bury Hill mansion which is of the mid-eighteenth century and later. The house was severely damaged by fire and has now been divided into separate dwellings.

There are several small houses and cottages along the lane. Little Trinity (No. 12) and No. 14, both built in 1840, are a pair of brick cottages in a simple Gothick style. No. 3 is tile-hung with some seventeenth-century brickwork and The Malthouse has a framed section that looks fairly late, probably seventeenth century. This is fronted with eighteenth-century mathematical tiles—one is dated 1724. Wyvern Cottage, next door, is a good brick house with a fine central stack and is late seventeenth century.

Above Wotton and Westcott, on the Downs, is Ranmore Common from which, like Newlands Corner and Box Hill, there are panoramic views. Here stood Denbies, the house Thomas Cubitt designed and built for himself in 1849. It was demolished in 1954, but the church, built for Cubitt's son in 1859 by Sir George Gilbert Scott, survives.

This is St Barnabas's. It is in a Gothic Revival style that is breathtaking in its complete abandon to rich elaboration, both in the use of expensive materials and in the carving of them. This is architecture which, for better or for worse, has conviction and confidence.

From Ranmore the North Downs Way turns northwards to West Humble where the ruined walls of an old, possibly twelfth-century, chapel remain opposite the barns of Chapel Croft. Beyond is the pretty Gothick Box Hill railway station. The North Downs Way then crosses the River Mole and the main Leatherhead to Dorking road to climb the slopes of Box Hill where we can pick it up again after looking at Dorking.

Dorking is situated at a crossing of the A25 and a north to south route from London to the south coast the A24 that roughly corresponds to the Roman Stane Street. The little Pippbrook Stream passes to the north of the town and once served the eighteenth-century Pippbrook Mill, no longer a mill but well restored and put to use as offices. The small, attractive nineteenth-century millhouse stands nearby, and the large mill-pond upstream is now a feature of a park.

From a distance the spire of Dorking Parish Church rises above the town and is very much a part of the scene, especially on the approach from the west and the high ground at Rose Hill and Cotmandene. However, it can be little seen from the main streets of the town, which is a great pity for it is one of the finer large nineteenth-century churches in the county.

The ancient church was taken down in 1835–7 and re-newed, all except the chancel. Then, in 1866, Henry Woodyer rebuilt the chancel, and in 1875 he rebuilt the work of 1835–7. The style is a version of Decorated and, unlike Scott's church at Ranmore, Woodyer's detail is re-strained. The interior is spacious, but without coldness, enhanced by the complicated roofs—more ingenious and involved than any medieval ones—and the pleasant colour of the mosaics of the late nineteenth century.

*St Barnabas's Church on Ranmore is an extravagant essay in Gothic Revival built by Sir George Gilbert Scott in 1859*

*St Martin's, Dorking, was built by Henry Woodyer in a restrained Decorated style. It is a striking feature in distant views of the town*

The West Street approach to the town has been under threat of change—the county council wished to sacrifice Clarendon House and the character of the area for the sake of what they considered to be necessary road improvements. Two public enquiries have now found against the desirability of making these changes, and Clarendon House, after being allowed to decay for several years, may even now be saved. One wonders to what lengths bureaucracy will go in its lavish use of public money even against the obvious wishes of local opinion.

It would be lamentable if this approach was spoiled as West Street, beyond, is one of the town's best streets architecturally, and has, incidentally, attained an international reputation as a centre for antique dealers.

No. 6 is a handsome weather-boarded house of the eighteenth century, and opposite is the King's Arms, a framed building that shows late seventeenth-century timberwork at the rear and at the side from Myrtle Passage. Then there is the Italianate Congregational Church, an impressive building erected in 1834. At the end of the street is a jettied row with a brick front in 1650 style, above modern but sedate shop-fronts. The gables have modern tile-hanging.

Possibly part of this row was owned by William Mullins, one of the Pilgrim Fathers who sailed on the *Mayflower* out of Plymouth in 1620.

West Street ends at a junction with North Street, the

High Street and South Street. In North Street there is more mid-seventeenth-century brickwork, including a brick mullioned window, besides a late sixteenth—or early seventeenth-century house, once the Old Gun, but, after ceasing to be a pub, it passed through a period of neglect. At the time of writing, however, the building is in the process of restoration. It has an oriel window on brackets with good carved detail. In North Street also is an old maltings, hopefully to be preserved, a brick in the walling carrying the name W. Attlee and the date 1854. Further north is Leslie House, a stuccoed and pinnacled building with square hood mouldings to windows that have nicely detailed Gothick arches worked into the design of the glazing bars.

Northwards again, down the sloping lane, is a plaque recording the waterworks of Resta Patching, dated 1738. The tanks of this early water supply were beneath the floor of the cellar at Brookside. The Patching family, members of the Society of Friends, were influential in Dorking for many years.

Dorking High Street, which rises from West Street and takes a wide curve past the White Horse Inn, is broad and could be impressive. It probably was once, but the modern blight of brash new developments and even brasher shop-fronts do nothing for it. A few good fronts remain, especially towards the narrower west end. These include a brick front of the mid-seventeenth century with an added double bow shop-front of the late eighteenth century and now an ironmongers. There is also the former 'Medical Hall', an early nineteenth-century shop with cast iron columns and balcony rail, which is very fine indeed. The White Horse is a complicated collection of various builds with an eighteenth- and nineteenth-century front to an earlier framed structure.

Dickens, who had associations with Dorking, placed the home of Sam Weller there and wrote that the "Marquis of Granby" was based upon the old King's Head (in the High Street where the post office is now). In the periodical, *All the Year Round*, he wrote that "the King's Head was a great coaching house on the Brighton Road in the old days, and where many a smoking team drew up when Sammywell was young."

On the eastern outskirts of the town is Pixham Mill, which is nineteenth century, and the earlier Pixham Mill Cottage.

To the south-east was Deepdene, the site of various successive properties including a house described by Aubrey and Evelyn in the seventeenth century. In the 1770s Charles Howard, later tenth Duke of Norfolk, built a late Palladian-style house there and this was the property that Thomas Hope bought in 1808.

Hope began improvements to it in 1818, inspired by his own knowledge of Italy and the Mediterranean and by the great wave of interest in things Greek that swept Europe

83

at that time. Deepdene became famous for its works of art, including the Hope Diamond, for its park and gardens and for its mansion and furnishings—all in the finest taste dictated by Greek ideas.

The fame of Deepdene continued during the lifetime of the son, Henry, but decline came in the early 1900s, and eventually the mansion was demolished in 1969.

On the Downs above here, we again meet the North Downs Way which winds past the great chalk quarries of the Dorking Lime Company that are no longer worked. Nature has taken over and has now mellowed the scene which has the character of a classical landscape by Claude: the small bridge that carries the North Downs Way over the quarry approach could have come from one of his pictures.

Buckland, a mile or so along the main road towards Reigate, with its church-like barn, is well known. The tower contains a water tank, and is a late addition to the barn which has a well-preserved roof of the late sixteenth century, little altered even by the insertion of the tower.

The nearby house, Street Farm, has later additions surrounding a framed house which, although externally refaced, appears by its roof structure to be fifteenth century, perhaps a little earlier than the barn.

Across the green is a very fine fifteenth-century hall house—now three dwellings—with a high quality crownpost roof. The roof truss that crossed the two-bay hall can be seen in the centre dwelling, and is finely moulded and comparable to the best of its kind, at farmhouse level, in the county. The building was once known as The Malthouse.

Buckland Church was virtually rebuilt by Woodyer in 1880. The bell-turret frame is old, but its pretty spiral stair inside, with Gothick detail, belongs to the nineteenth-century fittings as do the box pews and a font inlaid with coloured marble and with a carved wood cover. One of the nave windows has fourteenth-century glass claimed as the best of its kind in the county.

*Buckland Green, one of Surrey's best-known conservation areas, where the late sixteenth-century barn with its nineteenth-century water tower forms a picturesque group with Street Farm*

*The old Town Hall at Reigate forms a handsome focal point in the town. It was built in 1728*

CHAPTER SIX

# Reigate to the Borders of Kent

Reigate grew up around a castle that may have first been constructed by William de Warenne, created Earl of Surrey when he was granted the manor, probably by William II. An east-west route lay along the present High Street to the south of the natural sandstone hill—the site of the castle—and to the north of the old priory.

No masonry walls of the castle remain and the area is now a public garden. The old priory building has fared no better. It was founded in the early thirteenth century by William de Warenne, a descendant of the first Earl of Surrey, and his wife, Isabel, and at the suppression its numbers had dwindled to an Austin prior and three canons. Lord William Howard of Effingham obtained it from Henry VIII and probably destroyed the old buildings to make a mansion there for himself. This house was later demolished, or greatly changed, in 1779 when the existing Palladian front was built.

Old brickwork remains at the rear, some of which may be from the Howard house, but the feature of greatest interest is the so-called Holbein fireplace in the hall. This fireplace was reported to be *in situ* by Evelyn in his *Diary* (1655). It belongs to two periods—apart from minor later alterations and additions. There is the stone fireplace itself, and the large wood surround of flanking Corinthian columns. A date of about 1540 has been suggested for the stone fireplace and a little after 1560 for the surround.

At the western end of the hall is a massive staircase put in by Sir John Parsons in 1703. The woodwork, including turned balusters and panelling is of the finest craftsmanship and the walls and ceiling of the stair-well are covered with paintings attributed to Verrio. The design of the composition in relation to the stair-well is admirable, but the execution is indifferent.

Very little of fifteenth- or sixteenth-century Reigate remains: the continuous jetty houses in Slipshoe Street were a charming reminder of the late 1500s, but these have been spoilt by the application of a paint compound to the tiles.

Two eighteenth-century houses in the town are outstandingly good. The Barons, at the east end of Church Street, is about 1720 and is built in brick with the centre forming a slight projection. The doorcase is later than the house. Brownes Lodge, West Street, is later than The Barons: it is about 1780 and has a lighter touch that is conveyed by the use of decoration in Coade stone. The house

*Brownes Lodge, Reigate, dates to about 1780, it has an unusual triangular site and one of its 'fronts' enhances the entry into the town from the west*

is on a difficult corner site which adds to its interest by giving it two 'fronts'. The main entrance, in reality, is at the side and has a good porch.

The old Town Hall, near the junction of High Street and Bell Street, was built about 1728. It replaced an old Market House which stood on the old Market Place between West Street and Slipshoe Lane. The present building has been described as ugly—perhaps ungainly would be a better description. The arches and cupola seen from the south-east are a success, but the west end presents a pinched, uninteresting appearance although it is curved. The placing of chimneys at each corner was disastrous to the design because they compete with the effectiveness of the cupola.

The parish church of Reigate is to the east of the town centre and well sited in Chart Lane. It contains quite outstanding twelfth-century work in its north and south arcades, both of which have carved capitals in a Transitional style that is not quite so stiff as is usual.

The church suffered alteration in 1818 and restoration by H. Woodyer in 1845, and again—this time more gently—by Sir Gilbert Scott in 1877–81 when the nave arcades had to be rebuilt. The Reigate stone in which the church was built is notorious for its bad weathering qualities, and the church had to be refaced—Bath stone was used.

Redhill is a development on the eastern side of Reigate

and grew rapidly in the nineteenth century after the opening, in 1841, of the Brighton railway line. Before this the area was open farmland, and in twenty years, by 1860, it had outstripped the older town of Reigate in size and importance and developed a character typical of railway-orientated settlements.

Some early building remains in Linkfield Lane, and in Ladbroke Road there are some houses of the first decades of the nineteenth century.

There are one or two nineteenth-century churches, in particular St John's, first built in 1867, then remodelled on a large scale with a tall south-west tower and spire by J.L. Pearson in 1889–95.

Near the station is the Market Hall, built about 1860 in a mock-Jacobean style. The building was enlarged in 1891 and 1903.

Eastwards out of Redhill, the road climbs steeply and on the north side of the road, just before Nutfield, are Pimlico Cottages. They are in nineteenth-century *cottage orné* style with tall chimneys and ornate barge-boards.

Near here, on the southern side of the main road, is Nutfield Priory, built in the 1870s by John Gibson. This is a large house with a Tudor-style garden front. It stands on a ridge with the ground sloping away steeply to give extensive views across the Weald. The house is now a school for deaf children, and the best of the original house is carefully maintained.

*Nutfield Church which contains windows designed by Burne-Jones and executed by William Morris*

Near the village of Nutfield, which lines the A25, the church is well sited on a bend in a lane that descends to Nutfield Marsh. The tower of the church, with its short spire, is particularly impressive as one approaches it down the hill.

Below the church, towards Nutfield Marsh, are Peyton Cottages, a terrace of small nineteenth-century houses set back and at an angle to the road on a sloping site. Each cottage has its own individuality. Some are taller, some have dormers, but all have a feature in common—they are tile-hung. This welds the row together into an outstanding continuous, yet varying, design.

At Nutfield Marsh the large open green stretches away to the Downs where two miles away can be seen the mansion at Gatton. To the north-west are the quarries and plant engaged in the extraction of fuller's earth.

Bletchingley is about a mile east of Nutfield and stands upon the Greensand ridge south of the chalk Downs. The main road passes along the broad High Street which evolved on an extensive area to the south of the church where the market was held. Church Walk, now a narrow street parallel to the main road, was created by the building of houses on an island site in this large area.

Along this narrow lane are a former butcher's shop with a canopy that extends across the pavement, and a row of fifteen-and sixteenth-century houses, one of which is Wolmer Cottage (1552). From this lane one can see the backs of property in the High Street and at least one crownpost in a gable.

The High Street is lined on both sides with buildings of various styles and periods. Except for one or two eighteenth-century fronts, none are individually exceptional. Their value lies in their grouping. A great diversity of materials has provided texture and colour, which with an intricate interrelation of jetties, gables and roofs has fortuitously produced a composition of buildings of an excellence that no architect could possibly contrive.

The parish church of St Mary stands a little to the north of Church Walk. The massive western tower is Norman with later additions, but all the detail had to be renewed in 1910. The nave of an early church was replaced in c.1180, and the chancel was rebuilt in the thirteenth century when the south chapel was added.

Many alterations were made in the fifteenth century, and it was then that the south arcade was rebuilt. At this time also the chancel arch was built, the south arcade of the chancel was enlarged, and a north transept was added.

In the south chapel is a large marble monument of 1707 commemorating Sir Robert Clayton, Lord Mayor of London, and his wife. Their statues stand within an architectural frame of Corinthian columns supporting a curved pediment surmounted by urns, cherubs and angels. This monument, the work of Richard Crutcher, is an example of how British artists assimilated the spirit of the late Re-

*The row of houses built on an island site in the broad open space south of the church at Bletchingley*

*The White Hart at Godstone overlooks the green and village pond and is the result of successive changes and additions*

REIGATE TO THE BORDERS OF KENT

naissance in Europe and produced their own work with such confidence and a style they made their own, that they often exceeded the original.

North of the village is the site of the manor-house of Bletchingley, home of the Clares, lords of the manor until the last male heir was killed at Bannockburn in 1314. Henry VIII gave it to Anne of Cleves in 1540 when the manor was described as having a "splendid" house. Only a fragment of this is now thought to remain in Place Farm.

Brewer Street Farmhouse nearby is a large framed house with close studding—wall framing with closely placed vertical timbers. It has two gables at the front and a Horsham slab roof. One of the gables is a later addition.

Pendell Court, west of Brewer Street, was built in 1624 by George Holman whose son, Robert, gave the pulpit to the parish church in 1630. The house is in brick with stone-mullioned windows, and it has additions built in 1880.

Pendell House, further west, is a brick house of considerable interest. It was built by Richard Glyd in 1636 and is an example of a transition from a Jacobean house, with its central storeyed entrance porch, and a late seventeenth-century house with wide eaves cornice and symmetrical plan.

Godstone is interesting as it has two village centres, one at Godstone Green and the other at Church Town.

The route through the settlement near the church was used until the sixteenth century when it was bypassed by the easier, flatter route to the west that took the line of the old Roman London to Brighton road. The need for this may have been to serve a centre of the iron industry at Felbridge to the south, and another at Godstone called Hedgecourt which was owned by a John Thorpe in 1588. From about 1612–36 the Evelyn family also had gunpowder mills near Godstone. Whatever the reason, the old Church Town was superseded by Godstone Green which grew into a small town, and continues to develop.

Church Town is quiet and pleasant. The old church was comprehensively restored in 1872–3 by Sir George Gilbert Scott who lived near here at Rooksnest, now Ouborough. In 1872 he also designed the St Mary's Homes, south of the church, in a very picturesque style that made excellent use of the varying levels of the site in relation to the church.

Down the lane from the church are one or two framed cottages. Pilgrim Cottage is late sixteenth century; Tythe Cottage is an early hall house with additions including a large seventeenth-century chimney; and Pack House Cottage, another hall house, has a jettied crosswing. Part of it is early fifteenth century.

At Godstone Green, The White Hart is one of the most impressive buildings. A section of it was an open hall of about 1500, but extensive changes followed in the sixteenth century. The impressive south wing that has a great deal of exposed timber appears to have been extended piecemeal in the seventeenth century, and a yard was

93

created at the rear with an entrance arch into it that is now blocked.

The Godstone Hotel is part of another large house which appears to have been built as an inn in the later sixteenth century. The northern section is the oldest with additions to the south dating to the seventeenth century. A second block was added in the eighteenth century to form a double pile at the southern end.

The main A25 and the High Street are lined with a great variety of small buildings that in some cases contain

*The Bell Inn at Oxted with its impressive sixteenth-century jettied wing*

medieval work, but are mostly seventeenth century and later. The effect is similar to the one at Bletchingley and has resulted from the same combination of buildings to form a harmonious whole.

Like Godstone, Oxted, some three or four miles further east, has two centres. One developed along the A25 and the other, a mile away to the north, is around the old church.

The majority of the oldest buildings are not near the church but in the High Street which took all the A25 traffic until it was bypassed some years ago. This street slopes steeply down eastwards, and the ground also falls away to the north. As a result, the houses that line it are at various levels, many being built well above the road with steps up to the front entrances.

There are few other such concentrations of interesting houses in Surrey. Many were originally hall houses and have crosswings at right angles to the road. At the eastern end of Godstone Road, at its junction with the High Street, is the old dairy, now Nos. 2, 4 and 6, once a hall house with hipped roof and an eastern crosswing added. The Bell Inn, at the top of the High Street, is the most impressive with its sixteenth-century jetty fronting the street and running back down a lane sloping to the north. Lower down the street is another group of several builds, it includes Terrace Cottage and Huddle Cottage; Streeters is in the sixteenth-century crosswing that projects forward high above the roadway.

Apart from the early houses, there are later framed buildings several of which are brick-fronted. Some are eighteenth century—London House has a heavy eaves cornice of c.1700, and the George Inn and the Crown Inn, both of at least seventeenth-century origin, have modernized fronts that are not too much out of place.

Oxted Church is near a modern development that has grown up since the coming of the railway. It stands on a raised site in an almost circular churchyard which may have a pre-Christian origin. The west tower is Norman, built in ironstone rubble with sandstone dressings. The nave has evidence of twelfth-century work: shafts and carved capitals remain in the wall at both the north and south corners at the east end. In the fourteenth century the aisles were widened and at this time the passage from the north aisle to the chancel may have been made for use in processions.

Extensive work was done in the mid-fifteenth century when arcades, similar to ones at Lingfield, were put in, and the aisles were heightened. The porch is of this date and the escutcheons of the Cobham family of Lingfield are in the spandel of the arch, thus confirming a connection with this village.

There was a rood, and stairs that lead to the rood loft remain. Some cutting back in the stonework of the chancel arch also indicates its position. There is a faint fragment of painting on the chancel arch.

A restoration took place in 1637 when some external walls were plastered and the external mouldings of the east window were planed off. More work was done after a fire in 1719 that destroyed a wooden belfry on top of the tower and the nave roof. A north transept was added in the nineteenth century when much detail, including that in the tower, was renewed.

The official conservation area of Limpsfield extends in a narrow band containing part of Titsey Road and all the High Street that runs from the north-west to the A25 and across it to include the eighteenth- and nineteenth-century cottages in Wolf's Road and the village pond.

The village is a ribbon development in which, as at Oxted, the houses are built lengthways along the road, only crosswings being by necessity at right angles. There is no need here, as in a larger town, to conserve valuable frontage space and build end on.

Miles's butcher's shop is a charming and typical example of an early building with later additions and alterations. It was a hall house with a three-bay jettied crosswing. Changes were made when an upper floor was put in the hall and a brick chimney added in the first half of the seventeenth century. Later that century a three-gabled addition was made on the road frontage. The front of this addition was rebuilt in brick in the nineteenth century.

Eighteenth-century refronting is seen very clearly at Detillens House where a fifteenth-century Wealden-type house, with jettied ends forming a recessed centre, had a brick front added in 1736 after the jetties had been removed.

In Detillens Lane is a terraced row of cottages, the one at the corner with the High Street being a later sixteenth-century framed house built around a central brick chimney. The gardens of the cottages are across the road opposite where one old privy of a vanished row remains.

Old Court Cottage in Titsey Road is one of the important houses in Surrey. It was built about 1200 as a hall with aisles, very probably as a courthouse from which the Abbot of Battle administered his lands in Limpsfield. Many important features of an early date exist in this building. The carved capitals of the arcade posts are rare examples in wood of their stone counterparts, to be seen on the capitals of the Transitional churches of the early thirteenth century. The roof structure also is of an early form with parallel bracing and no longitudinal supporting purlins.

Limpsfield Church stands on high ground to the east of the High Street. It has a shingled spire on a Norman tower sited on the south side of the nave and chancel. The chancel was rebuilt early in the thirteenth century when the north-east chapel and south aisle were added. The Norman nave remains although altered by the building of a thirteenth-century south arcade and a nineteenth-century north aisle and arcade. An unusual feature in the chancel is the survival of an oven, with part of the flue remaining, for baking communion bread.

In the churchyard is the burial place of Frederick Delius, the composer, who died in 1934.

East of Limpsfield, and before crossing the Kent boundary, the last few hundred yards of the A25 cross the site of the London to Lewes Roman road. It then passes the Grasshopper Inn (modern fake Tudor), and goes through a gap in an early earthwork that appears to postdate the Roman occupation, but is not later than the ninth century A.D.

This great earthwork is most noticeable to the north of the main road, but it extends to both sides and gives the impression that it formed a barrier with only a narrow gap for the ancient roadway that can be identified south of the modern road.

The little group of farmhouses and cottages with one or two seventeenth-century barns at Moorhouse Bank are the last houses in Surrey at this point.

*The row of cottages in Detillens Lane, Limpsfield, with the privy to the right in the drawing*

*Woodmans Cottage in Park Road, Banstead, is typical of the weather-boarded houses of this part of Surrey dating to the late eighteenth century and nineteenth century. The timber-frame beneath the weather-boarding was often in softwood*

# CHAPTER SEVEN

# Banstead to Gatton

By tradition Banstead Downs has been a place for meetings either for sport or, on occasions, for more militant reasons as when the Surrey Militia mustered there in 1670. Horse matches were held on the downs in the seventeenth century, and at these the Duke of Monmouth is reported to have raced in 1678. Game was preserved and wardens were appointed to protect hares and partridges—the latter being taken with falcons.

From Epsom Downs, across Banstead Downs to the site of Oaks Park which gave its name to the famous race run in Derby Week, and beyond, almost to Purley, there is still some open heath and cultivated farmland. However, much building has been done in the area during this century and Banstead has a modern shopping street that serves the increased population.

Bordering the main street to the south is the parish church. Energetic restoration in the 1860s by G.E. Street renewed the external detail, and this work followed various repairs that were carried out in the seventeenth and eighteenth centuries. To what extent the building had been altered by this early work may not be known, but before the 1860s it is reported that the nave and chancel were in their "former state, much disfigured by big square pews". All this was changed. The interior, however, still has character. The piers of the early thirteenth-century arcades have simple capitals with plain volutes—only one of which is carved—and the nave roof, although altered to insert dormers, looks ancient.

In Park Road, east of the High Street, is the well. It is roofed by a quite considerable building that has recently been repaired and painted. Almost certainly erected in the eighteenth century, little is known about this attractive building which has fortunately survived the extensive redevelopment on the site of Well House which stood nearby.

Beyond the well are one or two interesting houses. Rosehill, built about 1730 with later additions, was originally a five-bay house that is now the section to the right of the present front.

Further along Park Road is a group of late eighteenth- and nineteenth-century cottages of which Woodmans Cottage, built about 1775, is a double pile, weatherboarded house containing much original detail including the doorcase.

Park Lane runs south-east towards Chipstead and de-

*Banstead Wood is one of Norman Shaw's houses and is now a hospital. It was built for the Hon. Francis Baring in 1884–90*

scends steeply past Park Downs and Banstead Wood to Chipstead Bottom.

The original house of Banstead Wood was built by Norman Shaw in 1884–90 and is now a hospital. It is a tile-hung house with large gables and tall chimneys. The bay windows are characteristic of Shaw and have casements incorporating semicircular headed windows within each unit.

Some three miles west of Banstead Wood is another mansion, Tadworth Court. This house was built in 1694–1704 for Leonard Wessels in a style associated with Wren. The architect is unknown, but the use of yellow brick—rather than red which was just beginning to pass from fashion—suggests a forward-looking architect.

Tadworth village is very much a downland settlement developed extensively around the railway which is on a spur from Purley that ends at Tattenham Corner. Westwards the commons extend across to Headley Common and Epsom Downs, still a sizeable open space.

Walton on the Hill is a mainly nineteenth-century and modern development with a few older houses around the church including a weather-boarded cottage in Breach Lane. In the grounds of Walton Manor, west of the church, is a mound or tumulus which could have been a Saxon motte later used as a meeting place for the manorial court.

Walton Manor now appears as a late nineteenth-century house, but it is, however, on an ancient site and contains fragments of a much older house. From what remains an interesting but rather incomplete picture of a large hall house and chapel can be built up. The walls are of flint with stone dressings for openings.

The chapel may not have had an upper floor as a remaining late thirteenth-century window on the north side appears to be too tall to allow for this. There are traces

*Tadworth Court, now a hospital, is well preserved and cared for and is one of the later mansions to be built in the Wren tradition*

*Chipstead Church is of Norman origin with twelfth- and thirteenth-century additions, but was heavily restored by the Aubertin family, father, and later, son, who held the living throughout most of the nineteenth century*

of an east window in the present attic.

In plan the hall stands back from the chapel so that only part of the south-east corner of the hall touches part of the north-west corner of the chapel. At this point there is an entrance between the two blocks. At the western end of the hall three doorways have been identified, two of which would have opened into service rooms, and the centre one would have led into a passage to an external kitchen.

The parish church of St Peter's has been restored, rebuilt, and added to so many times that little original work remains. There is a hint of former quality in the fifteenth-century nave, and there is a fifteenth-century piscina and sedilia.

A mid-twelfth-century lead font, possibly the oldest lead font in Britain, is, however, the greatest treasure. It is in the form of a frieze with eight seated figures in a Romanesque architectural frame of semicircular arches and bands of leaf patterns. The work was cast in a long band and joined to make a hoop. A break in the design at the join makes it obvious that a section, probably of four figures, has been removed at some time. The design is typically Romanesque: it is rigidly formal and well deserves the description monumental. However, fine as it undoubtedly is, I cannot join in the ecstatic praise that has been lavished upon it by some authorities.

North of Walton, and near Tadworth, in Sandilands Road, the site of a Roman villa was discovered by soldiers digging trenches in 1915. In 1948–9 the site was excavated and was found to have been occupied in the late Iron Age. Finds of pottery dating to the period a little before the invasion of Claudius in A.D. 43 have also been made. The site was re-occupied in about 100. Then, in about A.D. 250, a villa was built which was occupied until A.D. 400.

The choice of this site for a villa was obviously made because of the nearness of Stane Street—only two miles away. If he wished, a Roman would have been able to commute to London from his villa here almost as quickly, and often more comfortably, than his modern counterpart.

To reach Chipstead, the road through the valley of Chipstead Bottom is taken again. Then the route lies along the lane up the steep side of the chalk hill and leading to the village with its village pond and a fair sprinkling of seventeenth-century houses in the modern development of larger houses and tree-lined lanes.

Out on open downland east of the village and half a mile from the Reigate–Purley road, the church is beautifully sited in the slightest of hollows yet almost at the edge of ground that falls rapidly away eastwards. It is a beautiful place in the summer with a wide, open landscape and broad skies. Unfortunately, my visits there have too often been in the winter, and on two occasions I have had to seek shelter in the church from snow-storms.

As with so many Surrey churches, the story of Chipstead is of nineteenth-century restoration and addition. Its cruciform plan, with central tower, is of Norman origin, and in the twelfth and early thirteenth centuries the church comprised a chancel, a nave with south aisle, a central tower and transepts.

In 1808 the Reverend Peter Aubertin accepted the living, and finding the church in a state of neglect and disrepair, began a programme of restoration. Much of it was at his own expense and he acted as his own architect. He restored the chancel and built the south transept. In 1855 the nave was renewed.

More drastic changes came in 1883 when the son of Peter Aubertin—another Peter—held the living. The north wall, a survival of the Norman church, was taken down and a north arcade and aisle were added. An original doorway was salvaged and replaced in the new wall. The west doorway was also replaced at this time with the present modern one.

The church was built of flint, and Merstham stone—quarried in the valley below—was used for dressings, including windows, door openings. The use of this stone, so much liked by stonemasons because it worked almost as easily as wood and was a good substitute for Caen stone, has been the source of much regret. It weathers very badly.

At Chipstead the nineteenth-century west door is already decaying and the detail of the old resited north door has virtually gone.

Sir Christopher Wren complained of the unsuitability of this stone in his report on the condition of Westminster Abbey in 1713. He said that it was favoured for its easy working, but that "this Stone takes in Water, which, being frozen, scales off, whereas good stone gathers a Crust, and defends itself. . . ." Regarding the Henry VII Chapel at Westminster, which was also built of the stone, Wren said that its sad condition "begs for some Compassion".

Surrey churches may have suffered as a result of restoration at the hands of the Victorians, and their fabric may be crumbling through the use of unsuitable stone, but now there is something much sadder threatening them. It is robbery. Anything movable is at risk. The result is that many churches must be kept locked and often the search for the key is long and difficult. This obstacle, however, is not a bad thing: it could be a further deterrent to all but the boldest thief.

To set against this there is now a great revival of interest by parishioners in their churches. On occasions I have found churches open and literally buzzing with activity. At Banstead, Reigate and Merstham I found men and women turned out in force, ten or so of them, scrubbing and polishing floors and woodwork. One lady was high up on a ladder, undaunted in her efforts to remove dust from the rafters of an aisle roof.

The old quarries of Merstham were cut through for the new M23, and now with this highway, the old A23, the railway, and the bridges quite dramatic compositions are formed as these routes pass together along the valley near Merstham Church.

Still just a little distance away from the whirl of traffic, this old church stands on a hilly site, screened by trees through which vignetted views of the thirteenth-century tower and shingled spire can be seen.

Architecturally the present church is of thirteenth-century origin with north and south arcades and chancel arch. There is some large scale thirteenth-century blind arcading in the chancel, cut across by the Perpendicular arcade of the south chapel.

The most exciting feature of the church, however, is the west doorway. It is thirteenth-century work with dogtooth ornament within the arch, and shafts with moulded capitals and bases in the jambs. Inside the arch is a trefoil opening of unusual design: the upper section is not pointed but curved, like a horseshoe. The stonework was retooled during restoration in 1840, but it still survives as a quite perfect, simple example of what thirteenth-century stonemasons could produce, even for a village church.

Before continuing westwards to Merstham village and Gatton, a detour north-eastwards to Chaldon could be made, for at the tiny church there is what must have been one of the most remarkable early medieval wall-paintings in Europe—it is dated to around 1200.

As late as the 1860s Chaldon was reached only by trackways across the Downs, and by the great west to east pathway a mile to the south of the village centre. It is still remote.

The church is mainly late twelfth century in origin, and it was probably only a nave and chancel—the small window in the gable of the west wall dates to this period. When the church was enlarged by the addition of aisles around 1200, the large painting was also done. The tower and spire are modern, about 1843, and replace a small tower that was at the end of the north aisle. Two "belles in the steple" were listed in an inventory taken during the reign of Edward VI, but only one remains and is in the porch. It has been dated as not later than 1250.

It is reported that the painting was discovered by the Reverend H. Shepherd who saw evidence of its existence during the restorations of 1870–1. It was then carefully uncovered and restored. The subject of the work is the Last Judgement, with what has been described as the purgatorial ladder at the centre of the composition. The painting is divided by a horizontal band separating hell from purgatory. Heaven, the goal of the little people climbing the ladder, is depicted as a cloud in which is the head of Christ framed in a circle.

The drawing of the picture, as opposed to the content,

*Chaldon Church is remote even now and contains one of the most impressive medieval wall paintings in south-east England*

lacks all life and character, and it must be asked whether what we now see is but the 'ghost' of original work, carefully and neatly filled in and strengthened. The scenes portrayed are of great interest and illustrate many aspects of the ancient beliefs regarding heaven and hell—a picture story designed by the clergy to frighten the wits out of medieval illiterates.

The village has never been large, perhaps until quite recent times it consisted of only four or five farms and a few cottages.

In Dean Lane, on the way into the village from Merstham, on the B2031, the road passes an ancient framed house. It is, in fact, a fragment, the centre part of a fifteenth-century house with both its ends replaced by lean-to wings.

Chaldon Court, near the church, is, perhaps optimistically, dated mid-fourteenth century. It has a crownpost roof structure and was faced in flint and brick in the eighteenth century. Two large barns stand nearby at Court Farm. One, to the west, has a through purlin roof with angled struts and no collars. The principal posts have jowls, but the date is early seventeenth century. The eastern barn is somewhat later; it has side purlins, butted between the principal rafters, and placed 'not in line'. This structural form is datable to the last half of the seventeenth century, but could be found in early eighteenth-century work.

Rook Cottage, in the village, is thatched and is a sixteenth century timber-framed house with some later flint and stone walling.

Tollesworth Manor is south of Court Farm, near the 'Pilgrims' Way'. It was a hall house and is dated fifteenth century, but has many later additions and alterations including refronting in brick and stone.

Although there are very few old buildings a little character still remains in the village of Caterham-on-the-Hill that stands above a valley in the chalk Downs. One cottage, No. 84, High Street, is listed as early seventeenth century, it is part weather-boarded and has some traditional flint and brick walling. A larger house, No. 5–7, Townend, is dated 1640, and is entirely of flint and brick.

West of the village, off the Coulsdon road, is Caterham Barracks of 1877, it is a little forbidding and is surrounded by a wall of yellow stock brick. The entrance is dominated by a chapel designed by Butterfield in 1881. It displays his late style, but retains the polychrome work he was so fond of by using black with stock bricks together with flint. The interior has piers of limestone and red sandstone.

South of the village, and on each side of the road at the top of the steep descent into the valley, are two churches. One is of ancient origin and was replaced by the other for regular services in the nineteenth century.

The newer church of St Mary the Virgin, was built in 1866–88 in a 'correct' Gothic style that is frankly dull and over-large in scale.

The old church of St Lawrence opposite is of Norman origin. Part of the walls of the nave and chancel belong to this period and include a window in the south side where, also, a little of the Norman apsidal chancel can be seen, revealed by restoration work in 1927. The rectangular chancel was added in the thirteenth century.

The north aisle was added about 1190, and a south aisle was also built at about this time, and although destroyed, probably in the fourteenth century, the filled arches of the arcade can be seen in the south wall of the nave.

Restoration was done in the early nineteenth century when some uninteresting window replacements were made, part of the chancel rebuilt, and the west end stuccoed.

The frame of the bell-turret and the roofs are old work—the chancel roof is of sans-purlin type, and the nave roof is a crownpost construction.

In the valley below a new settlement developed around the railway that came in 1856 and which has not been extended further.

One of the first buildings at the rail terminus was a large railway hotel, but this has been demolished, as also has the original small station. An opulent mid-nineteenth century villa, No. 8, Stafford Road, and other less ornate houses in the valley, however, recall these early beginnings.

The Gothic church, St John's, was built in 1881, and was by the same architect who designed St Mary the Virgin. The Perpendicular-style tower of St John's, however, is exceptionally fine, possibly because the scale is exactly right for the site.

Other work in the town includes the Tandridge District Council Offices of 1912 in a bastard Classical-Tudor style that makes the building a period piece. Nearby is the Caterham United Reformed Church of 1874, in brick with stone dressings, it is a large building of mixed, possibly continental, ancestry.

The first hotel in the town was replaced by the present Valley Hotel in 1902 which is in a version of Norman Shaw's style. This building, together with the Grand Parade of 1903, indicates that Caterham was showing signs of expansion at the beginning of the century. Modern development of the shopping centre is not so decorative. It is a long, plain box-like block of shops totally without character that contrasts with the other side of the main street where, although there are no buildings of real architectural value, they do at least have variety, and the Old Surrey Hounds, with its fake timbering, adds a pleasant touch.

East of St John's Church is the telephone exchange, built in 1953. It is inoffensive, but has no guts and adds far less to the town than the unpretentious Miller Centre nearby with its lively juxtaposition of gables.

From the old church of St Lawrence, Stanstead Road

*A pleasant backwater, named after the play, Quality Street, but a difficult name for any street to live up to!*

*The Town Hall, Gatton, built in 1765, was the scene of the procedure of electing and declaring members of Parliament for this rotten borough*

leads southward to Arthur's Seat, and beyond, to Bletchingley. No. 179 a cottage along this road, is another example of the local flint and brick style. At Arthur's Seat, in War Coppice Road, is a nineteenth-century folly tower that is in an advanced state of decay, but it is very picturesque and must be worth preserving.

A little further along War Coppice Road is a brick water-tower of 1862, battlemented and very slightly reminiscent of Bishop Wayneflete's tower at Farnham.

The return to Merstham can be along the lanes from Arthur's Seat westwards along Quarry Hanger Hill.

Merstham is on the busy main road to Reigate. There are a few shops in the High Street, and near The Feathers is a mutilated framed house that looks to have been a quality building of the late seventeenth century, judging from an exposed section of nicely moulded beam. I wonder how this could have happened in a conservation area.

Quality Street is rather chic. It derives its name from J.M. Barrie's play *Quality Street*—Seymour Hicks and his wife, Ellaline Terries, were living in the street when they were acting in the play, which had its first performance in September 1902.

There is a varied collection of late seventeenth- and eighteenth-century houses in the street and some are as late as 1900. Home Farm has a group of farm buildings and a small granary on staddles. Court Cottage and Old Manor are sixteenth and seventeenth century respectively. Seymour Hicks's house was the Old Forge. This building is a fifteenth-century fragment which on close inspection can be seen to contain genuine work, but because it has been so much restored, at a distance it looks nineteenth century in a Norman Shaw style.

"Gatton is the most rotten of rotten boroughs"—this was how the village was facetiously described to me by the organist at Gatton Church who, after I had met him in the street and asked the best way to Gatton, conducted me there.

The borough of Gatton was created and given to Henry VI's steward in 1450 as a bribe in connection with the king's marriage to Margaret of Anjou, and it returned two members to Parliament until 1832. The Town Hall, which comprises a small classical Doric temple—with iron columns—was built in 1765 and was the scene of the procedure of electing and declaring the members.

The mansion in the park is a late nineteenth-century house built by Sextus Dyball for Jeremiah Colman, jnr, in 1891. It was severely damaged by fire in the 1930s and was rebuilt by Sir Edwin Cooper. The north front survived the fire and is now quite the best part. It has a large portico of Corinthian columns with marble shafts that contrast with the limestone of the building. The detailing is superb and very impressive. Several new buildings have been placed nearby for the Royal Alexandra and Albert School which now occupies the park.

Alongside the mansion is the tiny church of St Andrew. The origins of the church are ancient, but it was totally submerged beneath the extravagant attentions of Lord Monson in the 1830s. He filled it with good things, mainly panelling and wood carving, from a great variety of continental sources, and also gave it a very beautiful screen "from an English church".

Overwhelmed, I sat in the nave in a stall that had come from a Benedictine monastery in Ghent, and listened while my new friend played the organ—it needs frequent use, he told me, to prevent it from wheezing.

*Puttenden Manor is an early seventeenth-century house with a continuous jetty to which careful copies of old structures were added*

# CHAPTER EIGHT

# Farleigh to Burstow

The village of Farleigh is in the north-east corner of the country, just far enough south to be away from the urban sprawl of Croydon. It is at the edge of farmland on the gentle, undulating hills of the Downs.

Farleigh Church is one of the few churches in Surrey to have been carefully restored and to have little or no nineteenth-century additions. It was built in the twelfth century with nave and chancel of flint, then, in the thirteenth century the chancel was extended and lancet windows were inserted. Norman windows remain in the nave, and the west door is Norman. Only the chancel arch and the bell-turret are late additions.

South of Farleigh and deep in hilly, wooded country is the church of St Leonard, Chelsham. The church is remote now, but the small building just outside the churchyard is a reminder that it may have been even more isolated in the past, for it is a stable where the parson kept his horse and gig when he came to take the services.

The church was restored by an unsympathetic hand in 1870. A shaft and capital of late twelfth-century work in the south-east corner of the chancel are a sad reminder of what has gone—it may have been part of a wall arcade. Another, larger, and somewhat later, fragment of carved capital and shaft is in the opposite corner. This thirteenth-century work is contemporary with the piscina that has leaf decoration around its arch.

The chancel screen is a cut down parclose screen from a chapel in the south-east corner of the nave where there is a piscina. It is a very late example of sixteenth-century work and for this reason its introduction into the church during those troubled times following the Dissolution is all the more interesting.

Further south, but still on the chalk Downs, is Tatsfield. This is an old village that was developed in the 1920s. Upon first acquaintance it can be a little off-putting to find a small enclave of suburbia in so rural a setting.

Eventually one reaches the old village centre and the church which is on the edge of the southern slopes of the Downs where there are wide views across the Weald. The church has been restored and not too spoilt by additions, if the mean, pinched tower can be overlooked. The nave is Norman c. 1075 and has two Norman windows in the north wall. In the south nave wall are two lancets of the late thirteenth century: the one to the west has shafts and moulded capitals, but the other has an inserted square head

*Farleigh Church, carefully restored and containing little besides
twelfth- and thirteenth-century work*

of Tudor date.

The chancel was remodelled in about 1230 when two
lancets were put in, one on each side. The northern one is
the best preserved and has very elaborate mouldings together with shafts and moulded capitals in the jambs. The
east window in the chancel is similar to the south-west
window in the nave.

As the road descends steeply from the Downs towards
Limpsfield, it passes Pearson's Church at Titsey. It is not a
restoration, but a new church built in 1860–1 by the
ancient Surrey family of Leveson-Gower to replace a
former church. Unfortunately, I feel it does Pearson's
memory no credit; it is unfeeling, almost mechanical in
execution, but it has a magnificent site. Seen from the road
below, its shingled spire rises against a background of hills
and trees and it forms a fine group with Titsey Court and
Church Cottages nearby.

South of the A25, and bounded by the new western
border that now excludes Horley from Surrey, and by the
Kent boundary, is a flat area of Wealden clay. It is crossed
by the Eastbourne road, but by using the lanes in the area a
circular route can be taken that will lead to many places of
interest. This starts at the Tandridge turning on the A25,
continues southwards to the Sussex border, and returns
again to the A25 at Bletchingley.

The small village of Tandridge gives its name to the
Hundred and maybe this can be explained by the fact that

it gained some degree of importance when a priory was situated there.

A hospital of St James was founded at Tandridge about 1200. Soon afterwards this became a priory of Canons Regular of the Order of St Augustine. Their mission appears to have been to run a kind of hospice for the sick and needy, and their number, including the prior, is recorded as never exceeding five. At the Dissolution the priory was worth less than £200 a year and was dissolved under the Act of 1536. In 1537 King Henry sold the property to John Rede, and now little or no trace remains except the reported finding of some walling and the discovery of bones near the house now known as The Priory.

Tandridge Church stands upon the sandstone ridge that runs eastwards from Redhill, and south of it the village street slopes steeply down to flat Wealden country. In the churchyard there is a massive yew, its ancient limbs supported by props.

The church has been much restored by Sir George Gilbert Scott who also built the north and south aisles. The large timber framework supporting the bell-turret and shingled spire at the west end is of greatest interest. It has four massive cross-braced posts. Not all the joints are mortice and tenon, for some appear to be lapped. If this is so, then it would indicate an early date in the thirteenth or fourteenth century.

In the village the buildings are mostly of the eighteenth century or are modern. Flagpole Cottages, near the church, are pleasant, simply built in brick and are of two periods. The cottage to the north looks late seventeenth century and the other eighteenth century. Step Arbour Cottages, in a lane at the back of the main street, have some late timber framing and a large end chimney-stack.

Southwards, a little out of the village, is Brook Farm, an early eighteenth-century farmhouse. It has a good modillion eaves cornice and original sashes, and the quality of the brick front is exceptional. The use of blue headers to form a pattern in brickwork was exploited in the eighteenth century as well as by the Tudors. At Brook Farm a pattern has been formed by using English bond with rows of red stretchers alternating with rows of blue headers. Bright red bricks have been used for unusually tall arches above the window openings.

At Crowhurst there is another ancient yew tree similar to the one at Tandridge and the church also has a timber bell-turret and spire. This was rebuilt in the 1940s after a fire. The nave is of Norman origin, and the chancel is thirteenth century with a rebuild in the fifteenth century.

On the chancel floor is a memorial slab of cast iron with an inscription relating to Anne Forster, daughter of Thomas Gaynesford. She died on 18 January 1591. The slab is embossed with the kneeling figures of two boys and two girls, and in the middle is a shroud.

This casting is a reminder of the Wealden iron industry

and that it produced articles other than guns and gun-shot. Firebacks of many designs were produced in considerable numbers, and castings of the memorial plate of Anne Forster have been found used as firebacks. The inscription starting: "Here lieth Anne Forster. . . ." has led to strange beliefs when found on a cottage fireback by those who did not know its origin.

Anne Forster's father was one of the Gaynesford family of Crowhurst Place. They acquired the manor of Crowhurst in 1338 and a house at Crowhurst Place in 1418. The present house was erected in the mid-fifteenth century and was a moderately-sized hall house. It underwent various alterations, especially in the seventeenth century. After 1918 George Crawley made extensive additions and romantic modifications—the gatehouse at the entrance to the drive is his work.

Crawley was also responsible for work at Old Surrey Hall, near Lingfield, another house of *c.* 1450 that he remodelled with extraordinary flare, evoking a romantic Tudor dream-world.

Opposite Crowhurst Church is Mansion House Farm which is the result of several periods of building, much of it sixteenth century. In the mid-seventeenth century it was refronted in brick and has small brick gables and a very handsome porch.

From Crowhurst the road southwards leads to the Edenbridge road along which are Puttenden Manor and Haxted Mill. The history of the manor of Puttenden has been traced back to 1272 when the Lynde family held it. Later it passed to the Sondes family who retained an interest in it until the eighteenth century.

The present house includes high quality old work and some interesting early twentieth-century reproduction building.

In 1901 the estate was bought by the Honourable Mark Napier who, with his son, Philip, made many alterations and additions to buildings. This new work includes a large wing and the entrance porch. Mark Napier and his son followed a trend, current at the time, to build reproduction timber-framed buildings, and as a result they built a medieval Wealden-type house as a wing at the rear of the existing old building.

The front entrance is through their porch, and this leads to the kitchen which is possibly the oldest part of the house.

From the kitchen a door gives access to a large wing, an early seventeenth-century timber-framed structure which has a first floor, an attic, and at the garden front a continuous jetty and decorative timber work. The upper floor is gained by a newel stair, and another stair leads to the attic which was intended originally as sleeping quarters, probably for servants, and which was lit by windows in four gables that were removed long ago.

Two original chimney-stacks serve four carved clunch

*Haxted Mill, an eighteenth-century water mill with a gambrel roof*

*The approach to the church at Lingfield, with the building in which there was a medieval shop to left in drawing*

fireplaces, two on the first floor and two on the ground floor.

This is a very attractive house, and the skill with which the modern work has been done is an indication of the way such reproductions could easily pass for the original.

East of Puttenden is Haxted Mill, a large, timber-framed, weather-boarded double pile of the early eighteenth century with a gambrel roof. This roof takes its name from the use of gambrel to describe a horse's hind leg. Its main feature is a near vertical roof pitch to head height, followed by a pronounced reduction in pitch to the ridge. This provided much more space for storage than in a conventional roof. Its first recorded use was in 1547. François Mansard (1598–1666), the French architect, was responsible for later refinements of this principle.

Sterborough Castle, a mile or two east of Lingfield, was once the home of a branch of the powerful and influential Cobham family, but nothing of it now remains except a moat. Reginald de Cobham went to the manor of Sterborough a little before the end of the thirteenth century when he married the daughter of William de Hever. The son of this marriage, Reginald, succeeded in 1341 and was allowed to crenellate, or fortify, his house at Prinkham, later to be known as Sterborough Castle. He served in the French Wars, was at Crécy with the Black Prince and became the first Baron Cobham, dying of the plague in 1361.

His heir, another Reginald, succeeded. He was banished

*The old Guest Hall at Lingfield is a Wealden-type house but contains fanciful work put in by its restorer, George Crawley*

by Richard II, but returned to England with Bolingbroke, later Henry IV.

The third Baron Cobham, again with the Christian name of Reginald, inherited in 1403 and later became the founder and benefactor of The College of Priests at Lingfield, a college founded for priests to say Masses for the repose of his soul.

In 1431 the Abbot of Hyde at Winchester received royal licence to grant a perpetual advowson of the parish church of Lingfield to Sir Reginald and his heirs, and for him to found the college previously mentioned, together with a licence to convert the parish church into a collegiate church.

The collegiate buildings were erected to the west of the church, but nothing remains. In 1544, after the Dissolution, the Lingfield College estates were granted to Thomas Carwarden. As late as 1673 Aubrey visited the place and was able to describe the buildings. He wrote, "Near the church stood formerly a college erected by Reginald Lord Cobham, and dedicated to St Peter, for a Master and eleven priests of the Carthusian Order. I have seen no remains of any religious house so entire as this is."

The old Guest Hall of the collegiate church, at the north-west corner of the churchyard, is a Wealden-type house of around 1500—it can hardly be much earlier as it has a side purlin roof. Also, strangely, it has an obsolete crownpost standing on the tiebeam. This, however, must be one of the fanciful features that were inserted during the 1900 restoration. These also included a minstrel gallery—the romantic notion that musicians played while the lord and his guests dined is slow to die. It could hardly have been a regular occurrence and then only at great banquets. The house is now a branch library.

To the south of the church is a picturesque group of houses that includes Pollard House, which, like the old Guest Hall, is a Wealden house but much older, probably built during the first quarter of the fifteenth century. It has a later, early sixteenth-century wing in which there was a medieval shop. It was used as a butcher's shop until recent years.

The house facing the west end of the church is known as The College. It is not a part of the ancient college, but was built after Aubrey's visit—at least after 1680—and is a tile-hung, framed structure with butted side purlins in line.

Burstow is to the west of Lingfield in a very rural area of scattered cottages and farms with few village centres of any size. The church is down a narrow lane in a country setting of fields and large trees with only the rectory and Old Court nearby.

The striking feature of the church is the shingled west tower with pinnacles at each corner. An octagonal shingled spire rises from the tower.

It is difficult to accept this elegant structure as being sixteenth century, but it cannot be later. It is a combination of medieval skills in carpentry with a new feeling, not entirely Gothic, that strangely anticipates, however slightly, the proportions and grace of Wren's City church spires.

The nave and chancel of the church are twelfth-century Norman, but the chancel was remodelled in the fifteenth century when the south aisle and arcade were added to the nave. One Norman window remains in the north chancel wall and another in the north wall of the nave. John Flamsteed, first Astronomer Royal, was Rector of Burstow from 1684 until his death in 1719, and he is commemorated by a plaque on the east wall of the chancel.

Burstow Lodge, about two miles north of the church, is the oldest and most important building in the area. Like the Old Court it is on a moated site and probably had a drawbridge until the eighteenth century.

The date of the earliest part of the house is fourteenth century, and there have been later changes. It was built as a two-bay open hall house and was exceptionally wide. There is a limit to the span that is possible with a single oak beam, and at Burstow this limit has been almost reached. The medieval carpenter was not without the knowledge of roofing a wide building. The simplest way was to include aisles or to use a hammer-beam roof—such as the early one at The Pilgrims' Hall, Winchester, or the one at Westminster Hall—which achieved a wide span in a magnificent way and avoided the necessity of arcade posts.

With the use of a single-span crownpost roof at Burstow Lodge, the size of the main structural members had, of necessity, to be unusually large. The crownposts and their struts are massive, those of the centre of hall truss being at least some eighteen inches square.

At Smallfield there is a quite different house. Smallfield Place is one of the few good stone-built manor-houses in

*Burstow church tower, with its octagonal shingled spire, stands to the west of the church on four corner posts set on a stone base and forms an independent structure*

the country. It has a central porch with a gable and finials, the doorway has a four-centred arch and the bay windows are mullioned. Inside there is some contemporary panelling and a newel stair.

The house was built in 1600 by Edward Bysshe, a lawyer. His son, also Edward, was born at the house in 1615, and later became an M.P., Garter King at Arms, and Clarenceux King at Arms. He was knighted in 1661, the year he made alterations to the house.

Outwood, to the north is a small, scattered collection of cottages on heathland. Two windmills once stood there, but one collapsed some years ago.

*The impressive post-mill at Outwood dated 1665. The mill is pivoted upon a single post and turned above the round house when the sails were brought into the wind. The mill is no longer in use commercially*

# CHAPTER NINE

# River Wey

The River Wey and the River Mole are two of Surrey's main watercourses, apart from the Thames. Of the two, the Wey with the Wey Navigation has been of most value to the commerce of the county. It was a link with the Thames and London. Also, for a time, the Wey-Arun Canal was part of a canal system connecting with the English Channel.

The Wey enters the Thames at Weybridge, not far from the site of the Tudor palace of Oatlands which Henry VIII began building in 1538. He married Katherine Howard at the palace and spent much time there during his reign. Elizabeth was often at the palace, as was James I and Charles I. During the Commonwealth the old palace was mostly destroyed.

About 1725 a new house was built on another site in the park by Henry Clinton, Earl of Lincoln. His son, later the Duke of Newcastle, built the Broadwater and the grotto in the gardens. A fire in 1794 partly destroyed the house soon after Frederick, Duke of York bought it, and Henry Holland was commissioned to build a house in the Gothic style.

In 1857 the house was converted into a hotel by T.H. Wyatt and Holland's work was lost, only his entrance gate piers seem to remain. The Broadwater survives, but the superb shell grotto was destroyed in 1948—a great loss, and only a little walling of the Tudor palace remains in Thames Street.

Weybridge Parish Church with its tall spire is one of Pearson's early works. The interior is decorated with polychrome marble and some of the brasses are particularly good.

Opposite the church is a row of eighteenth-century houses that were associated with Portmore Park. In Thames Street are the remnants of the gate piers that led to this mansion which was pulled down shortly after 1835.

Hamm Moor is to the west of old Portmore Park, and since it is west of the river it is historically associated with Chertsey. The site of a moated house remains there, and at Hamm Court Farm, although itself a late building, there is a brick pigeon-house, probably sixteenth century, contained within later farm buildings.

Further west is Woburn Hill, a lovely, elegant, brick house of about 1815 with double-bowed front.

Brooklands, a house mostly rebuilt by Sir Reginald Blomfield in the 1890s, is in a very attractive Queen Anne style. It is now a college and is surrounded with dull schoolroom blocks.

From Brooklands the Wey flows past the old Brooklands motor race track, a short stretch of which can still be seen. It then curves around the eastern boundary of Byfleet. The canal leaves the river to bend to the west of the old village and is very popular with the boating people along the stretch from New Haw to the humpback bridge between Byfleet and West Byfleet.

Edward II must have been a frequent visitor to Byfleet as many documents were signed there by him. The manor was held by the Black Prince, and under the Tudors it was granted by successive kings to their eldest sons. Thus it was granted to Prince Henry, later Henry VIII, who annexed the manor to the Honour of Hampton Court. Elizabeth I visited the manor in 1576, and James I granted it to his eldest son. Then, after the prince's death, it went to James I's queen, Anne of Denmark.

According to Aubrey, Anne began to "build a noble house of brick". This would have been between 1612 and 1619. Aubrey left a sketch of the house on which he wrote: "begun by Queen Anne, finished by James Fullerton". He also mentioned a 'Ditterling Gate' and this is the gate still standing.

It is probable that the mansion was pulled down and the present house built in the late seventeenth century. Materials from the old mansion were used in the rebuild, in particular the pilasters on the front. Later work was done on the house in the 1740s or 1750s and additions and restorations were made in the nineteenth century.

On the river, near the manor-house, is the water-mill, much altered and now mostly nineteenth century. The Mill House nearby is a mid-eighteenth-century brick house with later additions.

Byfleet Parish Church, on the southern edge of the village, was completely rebuilt in the thirteenth century in a very simple style and was restored by Woodyer in 1864.

Beyond Byfleet the river passes Wisley where a farmhouse and small restored church of Norman origin make a delightful group. Then, past the gardens of the Royal Horticultural Society it joins the Wey Navigation.

The River Wey Navigation was built after an Act of 1651. The system joined the Thames at Weybridge and served Guildford, and then Godalming by 1760. The canal pre-dated the improvement of the roads and the coming of the railway and provided a valuable means of moving goods in and out of the county. The wharfs at Guildford are no more, but a treadwheel crane is still preserved in its crane-house near the river. The last commercial cargo carried was in 1969 and the Wey Navigation now belongs to the National Trust.

The Basingstoke Canal was open in 1791 and joins the Wey Navigation near New Haw. It was only moderately successful, and the last boat down to Basingstoke was in

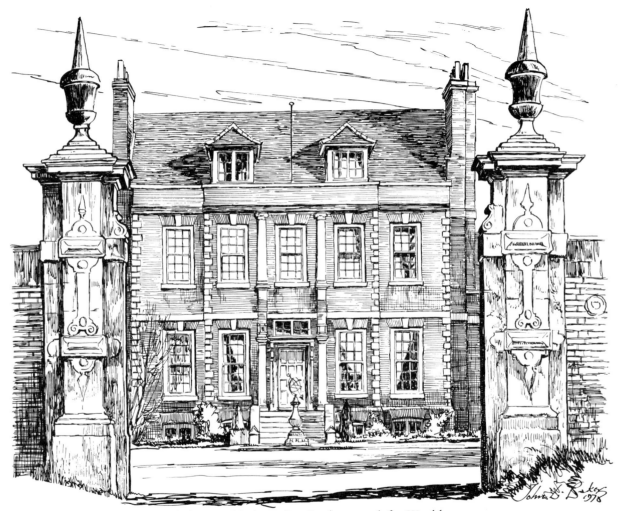

*Byfleet Manor House seen through the piers of the 'Ditterling Gate', so-named after Wendel Dietterlin, a German architect of the sixteenth century who 'invented' the style*

*Newark Priory in the water-meadows near the River Wey at Ripley, a house of the Austin Canons*

1914, the last one to Woking Gasworks was in 1936, and boats continued to bring timber to Spanton's wharf until the 1940s. Parts are now dry and overgrown, and there is a conflict between naturalists, who wish it to remain as a sanctuary for wildlife, and boating enthusiasts who would have it cleared.

The section of the canal bordering Woking could here, at least, be an asset to the town, but unfortunately Woking has fundamental planning faults in its new layout and such refinements cannot be hoped for. However, the use of Woking's large Victorian brick church, combined with the new town square, to create a traditional townscaped focal point, has been very successful.

From Wisley, the Wey and the Wey Navigation continue, sometimes in one course, often separately, towards Guildford. They pass some of the least spoilt stretches, Ockham Mill, Pyrford, Newark Priory, Old Woking, Send, Sutton Place, Burpham Court Farm and, finally, enter Guildford between Stoke Park and Bellfields.

At Pyrford the old church stands upon a cliff-like rise in the ground above the river valley and overlooks a landscape of open views—meadows dotted with trees, cattle and horses; open, but small in scale, a landscape one can know intimately.

The old church belonged to the abbey of Westminster until the Dissolution, so there were no resident secular lords of the manor to add chapels or make significant alter-

ations. In the fifteenth century the bell-turret was put in and it was probably then that the roofs were raised and renewed. There is a very good sixteenth-century porch with original barge-boards, and inside there are traces of a canopy of grace, or celure, that was once above the rood.

Wall-paintings from about 1200 remain, and the pulpit of 1628 was probably given by Nicolas Burley who lived at The Old House, Pyrford. This house still stands. It is of many periods and has a front of early eighteenth-century brick.

*The ancient church of St Nicholas, Pyrford, that overlooks the River Wey and Newark Priory*

*Woking Palace, once the home of Henry VIII's grandmother, survives now as little more than a few foundation walls and one small building*

Below Pyrford Church, near the river, are the ruins of Newark Priory. During the twelfth century a priory of Austin Canons was endowed at Newark, then called Aldebury, by Ruald de Calva and Beatrice de Sandes, his wife. The place became known as Novo Loco which became corrupted to Newark—New Place—and indicates that there was a previous site. The first settlement may have been at Ripley where the chancel of the church has some very fine twelfth-century stone carving, pre-dating work at Newark Priory by some forty years.

The Newark canons did not survive the Dissolution and little remains of their building except some picturesque ruins.

A short distance upstream from the priory, near the road bridge, stood Newark Mill until it was destroyed by fire in 1966. The destruction of so large and architecturally important a building was a great loss.

Many houses of interest are dotted through this area, but in particular there is Church House, which is just north of the church and has recently been carefully restored.

Upstream from Newark, is Papercourt Lock and, nearby, Papercourt Farm, a brick house of the mid-seventeenth century.

From Papercourt Lock to Old Woking and Send the river flows past the site of Woking Palace. This place was probably inhabited from quite early times, and a large house stood on the site, even in 1327. Surrounded by moats was a messuage incorporating a hall with a chapel. The most substantial part still standing is a small building with a barrel vault of brick, and ribs of clunch.

These are the forlorn remains of a mansion, once the home of Margaret Beaufort, mother of Henry VII. Margaret died in 1509 and the manor reverted to Henry VIII who succeeded to the throne earlier in that year.

Henry VIII was at Woking quite frequently, but succeeding monarchs took little interest in the mansion. Finally, in 1620, James I granted the manor to Sir Edward

Zouch who began the demolition of what was then a near-derelict property.

The manor again reverted to the Crown in Charles II's reign, and he leased it to the trustees of Barbara, Duchess of Cleveland, who died in 1709. She is believed to have held court in the village once—at the Old Manor House, a house with shaped gables and probably built with bricks from the old mansion.

*The Old Manor House, Old Woking, built in the later seventeenth century, possibly as a replacement manor house after the complete destruction of Woking Palace*

*Wey Cottage and Lea Cottage are seen to the left in this view of Old Woking Church from Church Street*

One would have expected there to be more good old houses in Old Woking than there are, but in Church Street, a cul-de-sac that ends near the churchyard, there are one or two houses that combine with the church and the modern lych-gate to make an attractive group. Wey Cottage and Lea Cottage appear to have once been a single house with a late crosswing, probably late sixteenth century, and an earlier, small, open hall structure.

The old Brew House, once also known as Magnolia Cottages, was a house of about 1718. There was evidence

*The old Brew House, Old Woking, built about 1718, it contained a superb contemporary staircase. The house was destroyed by fire in 1979*

that it had a heavy cornice typical of the late seventeenth and early eighteenth-century style. Inside, it had extensive panelling in several rooms, and the staircase, which was contemporary with the house, was one of the finest in the county. The house was severely damaged by fire in the summer of 1979.

Old Woking Church did not escape restoration in the nineteenth century, but there is still eleventh-century

work in the west and north walls, and in the west doorway under the tower which still has the original door reinforced with Norman ironwork of high quality. On the south side is a small seventeenth-century brick porch, now regrettably spoilt by its use as a boilerhouse.

Between Old Woking and Woking, at Kingfield, there is an important small, framed house of the early seventeenth century, Howards Farm, which was built with a smoke bay and has many original details, including windows. By the river at Send is Fishers Farm—mainly seventeenth century but with an eighteenth-century brick front.

At Send Court is a farmhouse of several builds that includes a hall house of the late fifteenth century and a crosswing of about 1580.

Send Church nearby was built by the canons of Newark as a chapel of ease and some thirteenth-century work remains in the walls of the nave and chancel. The tower is fifteenth century with some restoration, and the porch is early sixteenth century with good barge-boards. The nave is unusually wide and one wonders why this should be so in such an apparently unimportant church, and what kind of medieval roof it had—the present one is seventeenth or even eighteenth century. A fragment of a fifteenth-century screen remains and it can be seen that it turned down the nave on each side to form side chapels.

On the walls outside are some very good examples of

scratch dials made by the priests to time the saying of Masses.

Upstream from Send Court, the canal and the river pass Sutton Place, built in the 1520s by Sir Richard Weston. Then the river and canal unite, apart from a short loop to pass through Guildford. The other side of the town, at Shalford, the Wey Navigation and the river bend westwards to Godalming, and at this point also is the site of the former junction with the Wey and Arun Canal.

This canal was built between 1813 and 1816 and linked the Wey and the Arun Navigation, so giving an outlet to the sea at Portsmouth. It passed near Bramley and west of Shamley Green and Cranleigh to pass through Sidney Wood, near Alfold, out towards Loxwood and Sussex.

On either side of the route of the old canal the country is wooded and hilly, and mostly farmland. There are many cottages and farmhouses of the sixteenth to seventeenth centuries and some of the most unspoilt villages in Surrey such as Hascombe, Thorncombe Street, Alfold, Dunsfold, and Chiddingfold.

Bramley is a pleasant village with a stream passing through it. East Manor House is a late sixteenth-century house of several builds and with a stair turret framed with circle work. There is a late Lutyens house, Millmead, showing his later preference for classic motifs, and out beyond Snowdenham is Nurscombe Farm, a large, high quality, framed house. Built as a hall house, it later received first one and then a second crosswing in the course of its growth.

Further west, on the Godalming to Dunsfold road, is Winkworth Farm, another large mid-seventeenth-century house. It is sited below the roadway and stands behind a courtyard in a beautifully contrived setting that shows the combined influence of Lutyens and Miss Jekyll.

Near the line of the old canal is Whipley Manor, a large farmhouse with some early work contained within seventeenth-century additions.

Eastwards, on Smithwood Common, is Smithwood Farm, a fifteenth-century hall house with crownpost roof and later crosswings. Also on the common is Little Pittance, a small cottage which, like the larger Smithwood Farm, was built in the fifteenth century as a hall house.

Cranleigh is a large village with the remaining older buildings rather swamped by pleasant enough nineteenth-century development and modern expansion. There are some interesting houses on the green including Mercers Cottage, a particularly good fifteenth-century hall house. A modern shopping precinct has pretensions to being in a 'Georgian' style, but has failed miserably in matters of proportion and detail. Opposite this is a row of cottages and houses, some of the sixteenth and seventeenth centuries, concealed by shop conversions.

The church, was restored in 1864–6, but retains some original thirteenth and fourteenth-century work includ-

*Little Pittance on Smithwood Common, a small two-bay hall house with crownpost roof*

ing the carving of a grinning cat said to have inspired Lewis Carroll's Cheshire Cat. The striking fourteenth-century tower of the church, built in carstone and a conglomerate called pudding stone, has unfilled putlock, or scaffold holes, an unusual survival.

Cranleigh was one of the centres of the iron industry in the Weald. Vachery Pond, south of the village, was constructed to supply water to the Wey and Arun Canal and is at a higher level than the old hammer ponds that are shown on seventeenth-century maps.

The production of iron in the Weald dates from pre-Roman times. The methods then used were by the direct process that produced wrought iron immediately ready for forging into tools. This process continued until the introduction of the blast-furnace from France at the end of the fifteenth century.

A blast-furnace produced cast iron in a fluid form that could be cast into moulds, but was converted into wrought iron only by treatment at the forge by the use of the hammer. The process required an outlay in capital for buildings and maintenance and it attracted and created wealth. The houses of the iron masters reflect their prosperity as is seen at Burningfold Farm and Lythe Hill Farm (now a hotel).

The power required was provided by water, and the so-called hammer ponds were created by damming the small Wealden streams. The charcoal fuel came from the local

*The massive tower of Cranleigh Church demonstrates Surrey's lack of good building stone by the considerable use of pudding-stone in its construction*

forests.

During the sixteenth century the industry prospered, waxing and waning with the demand of the munitions trade for cannon. It is said the first cannon to be cast (as opposed to wrought) in the Weald was made at Buxted in 1543.

An interesting minor product of the industry was the casting of firebacks to protect the bricks in domestic chim-

*Alfold House in which the colour and textures obtainable by the simple use of traditional materials is superbly shown*

neys, and there is a fine collection of these at Petworth House.

Competition from imported iron, the introduction of coal-burning blast-furnaces at Coalbrookdale in 1735, and the establishment of the Carron Ironworks in Scotland in 1760, all proved too great for the Weald. The increasing cost of the charcoal—the importation of coal was not practicable—and the limitations of power dependant upon water supply caused the industry to run down. One of the last ironworks to close was at Fernhurst, just over the Sussex border. It was run by John Butler and produced cannon until 1790.

Moving southwards, near Alfold Crossways, is Bookers Lee, a late sixteenth- or early seventeenth-century framed house with ogee braces—and a small pigsty, a rarity now.

On the approach to Alfold from the Crossways is the lovely Alfold House, built in the later fifteenth century as a hall house. The large original front doorway remains, as does the cross passage behind it and the doorways off it into the old service end. At the high end of what was once the hall, can still be seen the master's doorway into his parlour. There is a superb crownpost roof above the old hall and another above the crosswing which must have been built very soon after the hall because of the similarity between the two.

The church at Alfold and the cluster of cottages near it form one of the many attractive groupings that seem to

*Tile-hung cottages and shingled church spire at Alfold make a typical Surrey scene*

*Oak Tree Cottage is a hall house with a crownpost roof and smoke deflector. The crosswings are later additions*

occur naturally in Surrey. The church has a late twelfth-century south arcade and a fourteenth-century north arcade. A large crownpost roof of late fifteenth-century appearance runs into the massive sixteenth-century framework that supports the bell-turret and shingled spire. The font is eleventh century: a simple barrel shape with incised arcading around it in which there are low relief crosses. The base is finished with a band in the form of a cable.

The lane behind the church leads to Sidney Farmhouse, a mid-sixteenth-century hall house, and to Sidney Wood where one of the Wey and Arun canal superintendent's houses still stands.

Sites have been found where the glass industry developed in the wooded country here on the borders with Sussex. The industry appears to have begun as early as the thirteenth century and by the mid-1300s it was flourishing. By 1615 glass manufacture in the Weald had ended with the prohibition of the use of timber for the furnaces.

At Dunsfold, apart from Burningfold mentioned earlier, the Old Forge is quite exceptional. It was an aisled hall house with a roof construction of parallel bracing. Its date is probably thirteenth century—making it one of the earliest houses in Surrey.

Oak Tree Cottage, which is mid-fifteenth century, is another hall house, but with a rare form of deflector in the roof that directed the smoke from the open hearth in the hall, out through the gablet. One other example is at Lee Crouch, Shamley Green referred to in Chapter 4. Cross-wings were added, one in the seventeenth century and the other later, and a brick front was added in the early eighteenth century.

Dunsfold Church, built in 1270, has been restored very little and the original church remains almost complete. Its high quality may be attributed to its being in the advowson of the Crown at the time of building. Most of the pew ends are original thirteenth-century work, simple in design, but very fine. The bell-turret is supported on a heavy timber structure, like those at Alfold and Thursley.

At Chiddingfold, westwards through the lanes that here seem so remote, is the Crown Inn, a Wealden house with the characteristic jettied ends that create an apparent recessed centre. This house, which has a high quality crownpost roof, probably dates to the late fourteenth century and is the house referred to in a document of 1383.

Chiddingfold has many tile-hung cottages around the large green and along the road curving down to the bridge where there is an interesting fragment of another Wealden. Above the Crown is a striking mid-eighteenth-century building, Old Manor House, with a good Tuscan doorcase.

West of the village is Combe Court Farm, a fifteenth-century hall house, tile-hung, and with seventeenth-century additions. It has an important range of Victorian farm buildings, tile-hung and in a picturesque

*The Crown Inn at Chiddingfold appeared as a tile-hung jetty house until restoration revealed it to be a Wealden house*

Gothic style. Hawlands, to the south, is a continuous jetty house of the late sixteenth century, and at nearby Killinghurst is a superbly-sited large house, built in 1760 and grand in a truly rural setting.

Near Killinghurst is Imbhams, an ancient manor where there was once an iron furnace, the property of the Quenell family of Lythe Hill. It was probably Robert Quenell who built the very decorative timber-framed wing to the house now called Lythe Hill Hotel. Robert's son, Peter, was a Royalist and cast guns at Imbhams for the king.

Haslemere, a medieval borough, is now a busy small town, and has grown with the surrounding district, especially since the nineteenth century when many large houses were built. The main street of the town is set against a wooded, hilly background to the south, and terminates in a brick Town Hall built in 1814.

A few old buildings remain on the east side of the street, including the mid-eighteenth-century White Horse Hotel, but much has been replaced in the last hundred years. The Georgian Hotel, as its name implies, is mid-eighteenth century but it has many later additions. Town House, in lovely early eighteenth-century brick but with a later upper storey, and the museum are at the northern end of the main street.

Southwards from Lower Street is Shepherds Hill where there is a group of small houses of varying dates and styles standing above the steeply rising road.

To follow the western branch of the River Wey, and the Godalming Navigation, it is necessary to return to Shalford. The building of the canal, that in part follows the course of the river, was completed in 1764 and was an important link with Guildford that assisted in bringing prosperity to Godalming. Beyond Godalming the river continues westwards, with one branch to Farnham, and another to Frensham.

The story of the Wey from Guildford to Farnham can be connected with that of the medieval stone bridges that cross it. Eighteen of these bridges are known to have been built, including ones at Guildford and Godalming, and it is reasonable to suppose that they were built by the monks of Waverley about the mid-thirteenth century as part of their road system to outlying granges.

The Guildford bridge was altered in 1760 to allow the passage of canal traffic. Then in 1900 floods brought down the centre arch and the rest was demolished. Of the three original bridges at Godalming only the Westbrook Road bridge incorporates old work.

At Unstead the course of the river has been changed, but the old bridge remains still carrying a considerable flow of traffic. Like all the others in the group, it has cutwaters: those facing upstream being pointed while the downstream ones are rounded to minimize the effect of eddying water on the foundations.

Standing near this bridge is Unstead Farm, a fine example of a good quality, larger fifteenth-century farmhouse, the older parts of which include a two-bay open hall with a moulded centre of hall crownpost. An upper floor was inserted in the hall and a crosswing was added, probably at the same time, in the early seventeenth century. Two very good crow-stepped brick chimney-stacks also belong to this period.

Above Unstead Farm is Upper Unstead Farm, another hall house originally, but of a later date—about mid-sixteenth century. It also has a good quality crosswing

*Unstead Farm now survives as a late fifteenth-century hall house with an early seventeenth-century jettied crosswing of high quality*

*Eashing Bridge, one of the series of bridges over the River Wey that were probably built by the monks of Waverley Abbey*

with a reliable date of 1665 cut on one of the fireplace bressumers.

Upstream, the river and canal pass Catteshall Mill, now rather ruinous. Near the mill is The Ram cider house which was originally a hall house of the later sixteenth century. It was built with half of its two-bay hall floored and is an example of an intermediate stage between the open hall and fully-floored house. Features of the service end remain, but the parlour end was altered long ago.

At Godalming the Wey is crossed by the old Portsmouth Road, and upstream is Eashing where there are two of the old Wey bridges, repaired by the architect Thackeray Turner and given to the National Trust which also owns the cottages nearby.

West of Eashing, the A3 passes over the river and upstream is Peper Harow Park, once the home of Viscount Midleton. The house was built in the 1760s by Sir William Chambers, but has been spoilt by the addition of later work, especially the large entrance porch. The stable block is particularly good and is extravagantly built in Bargate stone cut to brick size and laid as brickwork.

Peper Harow Church was restored by Pugin in the 1840s and his imaginative reconstruction of a church of several periods compensates a little for the loss of original work.

The large complex of farm buildings near the church includes a very large granary, a late seventeenth- or eighteenth-century example of good timber construction using imported softwood for the larger timbers.

On the southern edge of the park is Oxenford Grange where Pugin built a 'ruin' and also a small range of farm buildings that includes a stone barn that is as honest and workmanlike as any medieval work.

Westwards again, at Elstead there is another old bridge. Elstead still has some old cottages around a village green, but the Old Farm House, between the river and the green, is a high quality hall house with later additions, one of which includes an eaves cruck, a rare feature in Surrey, and similar to the one at Littleton, near Guildford.

Upstream from the bridge there is a large eighteenth-century mill surmounted by a cupola and with an adjoining eighteenth-century brick mill house.

At Tilford, a mile or two upstream, the river divides and old bridges cross both watercourses, one of which flows down from Waverley and Farnham, and the other from Frensham.

Waverley Abbey, on the Farnham branch of the river, has been described in Chapter 1. There were at least two bridges between Tilford and the abbey, besides two more near the abbey precincts. Beyond Waverley there were a further two bridges before Farnham Bridge—this was replaced several times and is now an iron structure.

The south-western arm of the river meanders through wooded country to reach open, heathland at Frensham where the Great and Little Ponds are an attraction, particularly to dinghy sailors. The country hereabouts, and across to Hindhead, was favoured by nineteenth-century builders of large houses, Norman Shaw's Pierrepont, built in 1876 in his typical late picturesque style, is probably the best of them.

*Peper Harow Granary is a large seventeenth-, or eighteenth-century, building in which imported softwood has been used*

CHAPTER TEN

# The Portsmouth Road

The Portsmouth Road—there is a ring about it. One can visualize the shining coach with its four blood bays tossing their heads with impatience as they wait for the 'off'. For thirty years from the beginning of the nineteenth century, the Augustan Age of the English road, such scenes were frequent daily occurrences along the Portsmouth Road.

From London the road went through Kennington, Battersea Rise, Wandsworth, up to Putney Heath at Tippets Corner and, joining the West End coach road that had come across Putney Bridge, went down through Kingston Vale into Kingston-upon-Thames, eleven miles out of London and the first stage.

In 1749 the road was turnpiked from Kingston to near Liphook and toll-gates were erected at Cobham, Ripley and Farncombe—this gate was moved close to Guildown in Guildford in 1767 and did not go until 1870.

Out of Kingston, the road went across Ditton Marsh into Esher and the second stage was completed at The

*St George's Church, Esher, where an outside stair leads to the Newcastle Pew that was used by the unfortunate Princess Charlotte during her brief residence at Claremont*

Bear. Externally The Bear has probably changed little since the early nineteenth century, but the extensive stabling, once claimed to be large enough for a hundred horses, has quite gone.

The little church of St George's, behind The Bear, still stands with its memories. Inside there is an eighteenth-century three-decker pulpit, a reredos of 1722 and a west gallery of 1840–2, but the most interesting feature is

*Waynflete's Tower at Esher built as part of a courtyard house in the 1470s and overlaid with Gothick detail by William Kent in the eighteenth century*

the Newcastle Pew, probably built by Sir John Vanbrugh about 1725.

A map of 1606 shows the old manor-house of Esher down by the River Mole and, like many important medieval houses of this type, it was arranged around a courtyard and entered through a gateway. This gateway alone remains. Known as Waynflete's Tower, it was built by Bishop Wayneflete of Winchester in the 1470s, about the time he was building the similar tower at Farnham Castle. It is in brick, simpler than the Farnham one, but has a newel stair constructed entirely in brick—a staggering display of bricklaying skill.

In the eighteenth century the park, and the old manor-house of the bishops of Winchester were separated, and in 1708 Vanbrugh purchased ground on the southern side of the Portsmouth Road. He built himself a house there, but sold it, in 1716, to Thomas Pelham, later Duke of Newcastle. Then in 1729 Henry Pelham, the statesman, acquired the old manor-house.

From contemporary engravings it can be seen that the old gate-house was incorporated in new buildings built for Pelham by Kent, and was transformed into a small mansion in the Gothick style. The detail added to the gate-house by Kent remains in door and window openings and mock vaulting inside.

The old manor-house site was abandoned for another where Esher Place now stands, and all except the gate-

*The house built for Clive of India at Claremont, near Esher, by 'Capability' Brown*

house was demolished. Thus it remained, almost a ruin, until Frances Day, the actress, repaired it and made it habitable.

In the park on the other side of the Portsmouth Road, Vanbrugh's house purchased by Thomas Pelham, was added to and improved. On a mount at the rear of the house Vanbrugh built a garden house, a belvedere, which pleased the duke so much that he combined his title, Earl of Clare, with mount, and called the property Claremont.

The gardens of Claremont were famous. They were first laid out by Charles Bridgeman, better known for his Round Pond at Kensington, and they included a lake and an amphitheatre. William Kent, who had worked on the old manor, was employed next to remodel the gardens in the 'naturalistic' style which his genius as a landscape-gardener had helped to make fashionable.

In 1788 Clive of India bought the estate from the Duke of Newcastle's widow and he built a new house sited on higher ground; this is the house standing there today. It is in the late Palladian style and was designed by 'Capability' Brown whose firm, Brown and Holland, employed the young John Soane.

After the death of Clive, the house passed through several owners until, in 1816, Princess Charlotte, daughter of the Prince Regent, later George IV, was married to Prince Leopold of Saxe-Coburg and she was given the house as a wedding gift from the nation. The young princess died eighteen months later, but Leopold continued to live there, for a time.

In 1931 the mansion, including the stables and the belvedere, were acquired by the Claremont School Trust Ltd. The National Trust purchased the neglected lake and woodlands south of the house in 1949 and in 1975 began the now completed restoration of the eighteenth-century gardens.

Out of Esher village, past the entrance to the National Trust Claremont gardens, the road goes up to the Fairmile, the only straight and level section between London and Guildford, and on to the White Lion at Cobham. In the 1820s this inn did considerable trade with private posting travellers and Postboys Row, a terrace of nineteenth-century cottages nearby, recalls the great days of the post-chaise—and stage-coach.

From the White Lion the road continues up the hill towards the lodges of Pains Hill. Near here, where there is a small housing development, was the cottage where Dr Matthew Arnold lived in retirement. A bridge once passed over the road at this point, and when recent road-widening schemes were in progress, part of this bridge was revealed in the bank.

From the road here, part of the old Pains Hill House can be seen, just inside the present park wall. This was the house around which the Honourable Charles Hamilton created a park from about 1738, a park that was one of the minor wonders of the age. He improved the fertility of the ground and established a vineyard; he made a lake—with islands cunningly contrived to make it seem much larger than it was. As one walked through the park, new vistas constantly opened up, with the added interest of a ruined abbey or a temple and a grotto by the lake.

Many of these architectural embellishments have gone, but the Gothic Temple—or Pavilion—and the ruined abbey just about survive. The portico of the Temple of Bacchus is now incorporated in the rear of the present mansion.

Part of the park is in the hands of Elmbridge Borough Council, and as I write, there are negotiations to purchase the remainder. It may not be too late to recreate just a little of the exciting landscape made by Hamilton.

At Pains Hill the old Portsmouth Road meets the new road that cuts across the landscape from the Kingston By-pass towards Guildford. The old road passed through Ripley where The Talbot was the third stage, and during the eighteenth century and the early nineteenth century Ripley grew because of the importance of this staging point to the surrounding district.

There are several late medieval buildings in the village. Vintage Cottage, in particular, is a house that can be compared to the widow's cottage described by Chaucer in *The Nonne Preestes Tale*: "Sooty her bower and her own small hall". The hardware store near The Ship may be equally

*The Anchor at Ripley, a timber-framed building of various dates, a popular rendez-vous for cyclists at the beginning of the century*

ancient—part of it has a crownpost roof like the one at Vintage Cottage.

The Anchor is another old building that is of interest and The Talbot has a large mid-eighteenth-century front and coach entrance, but this conceals quite a considerable framed house at the rear.

The growth of the village in the eighteenth century produced many new brick houses. The Clock House is a nice example and shows the use of black header bricks, that

147

*The broad main street at Ripley on the Portsmouth Road once the scene of the busy coaching trade and still not much relieved from modern traffic by the new bypass*

were probably specially glazed, to produce a pattern. At the northern end of the village, Rydehouse, which belongs to the latter part of the eighteenth century, is of fine quality, and nearby is Footbridge House, a timber-framed building refronted in brick.

In the 1890s the bicycle was a popular means of escape and recreation for people living in the built-up suburbs of large towns and cities. A ride along the Portsmouth Road as far as Ripley was a favourite trip for London cycling clubs, who patronized the local teashops and pubs, including The Anchor.

From Ripley the road goes past the gate-house of Sutton Place, the mansion built soon after 1521 by Sir Richard Weston. It was originally constructed as a courtyard house but the northside, with a gate-house, was demolished in 1786. It was an unfortified mansion, very much of its period, with Italian and Gothic detail mingled. The doors and windows retain Gothic cusps and mouldings, but are surrounded by panels of terracotta *putti* and other Italian motifs.

Passing Sutton Place, the road continues to Burpham and enters Guildford through nineteenth-century suburbs to the north-east. Out of Guildford the road climbs steeply towards Godalming and crosses the North Downs Way at St Catherine's, near Braboeuf, a Victorian Tudor mansion built around a manor-house said to be sixteenth century.

Beyond St Catherine's is Artington, where Old Friars, a house near the road, has a gable with curved braces, forming quatrefoil patterns. The gable looks late sixteenth century, but is, in fact, modern—not later than mid-nineteenth century—and the gable is duplicated at the garden front. Apart from a quite ordinary wing of the late seventeenth century, the house is an exceptionally good crownpost, open hall type of around 1500, or a little earlier.

The great house of Loseley, built between 1563 and 1569, and the village of Littleton are to the west of Old Friars and can be reached on the loop road starting at Sandy Lane, St Catherine's.

There are several framed houses in Littleton. Willowmede is mid-seventeenth century and there is Pillarbox Cottage, Little Cottage, Church Cottage and Long Meadow. All combine delightfully with the little St Francis Church and the nineteenth-century school. However, the most interesting house, now known as Nos 8 and 9, is timber-framed and may be mid-fourteenth century. The roof is of early construction having no purlins, but the feature of greatest interest is the pair of eaves crucks in the end of the house nearest the road—a rare feature in Surrey.

Loseley House is still the home of the descendants of its builder, Sir William More, one of Elizabeth's trusted supporters in Surrey. The original plan for the house was for three wings with the fourth side closed by a wall and a gatehouse. It is not certain whether the scheme was fully carried out, but in the 1560s the present wing, and a north-east wing, were erected. The north-east section fell into disrepair and was demolished in 1835.

It is fortunate that the remaining wing contains the principal rooms, particularly the great hall, now entered from the screens passage. The doorcase of the main entrance belongs to improvements of 1689 which also included the embellishment of the original oriel window at the high end of the hall. The door was then placed in a new central position in relation to the hall, but in the nineteenth century it was moved to its present position, the original entrance into the screens passage.

The late Tudor appearance of the hall is achieved by a miscellany of items from different sources. The belief that the panelling came from Nonsuch is now not completely accepted, but the interior provides the ideal setting for the painting of Sir William More-Molyneux with his wife Cassandra, and eight of their children, painted in 1739 at Loseley by Somers.

The sixteenth-century carved chalk fireplace in the drawing-room is one of the largest of its kind and is believed to have been cut from one block.

At Farncombe, a suburb of Godalming that sprang into life when the railway arrived, are some old buildings, notably the Wyatt Almshouses, built in 1622 by Richard Wyatt. They are in red brick and have a very effective row of tall chimney-stacks at the rear, broken by the central gable of the chapel.

On the hill above Godalming is the school, Charterhouse, built in 1872 by P.C. Hardwick. There are additions by Blomfield (the Great Hall); Sir Giles Gilbert Scott (the Chapel); and James Dartford (the Art School). Probably the best of its kind in the country, the large complex is a combination of symmetrical plan with asymmetrical elevations and detailing which enlivens the composition and adds a picturesque note.

The Portsmouth Road enters Godalming across the late eighteenth-century bridge built by the County Surveyor, George Gwilt. The bridge spans the River Wey and the view here across the meadows can be quite beautiful. The expanse is large enough to produce dramatic effects of light, or, on quiet days, a gentle setting for the church and its tall, slender spire which, with the fields, trees, river and surrounding hills, composes into a score of pictures.

Narrow Bridge Street curves up to join the High Street at its junction with the road from Hascombe. The imposing King's Arms, a coaching inn built in 1753, dominates this end of the High Street. The Emperor Alexander I of Russia and King Frederick William of Prussia dined there in 1814. Peter the Great of Russia was also a guest at Godalming in 1698 when he stayed at Moons, an older house on the site of the King's Arms and named after its owner, James Moon.

*Loseley House, built by Sir William More in the 1560s partly with material from Waverley Abbey*

*The Town Hall, Godalming, replaced an older building in 1814. It is affectionately known as the Pepper Pot*

Some character has been retained in the High Street and in the town as a whole. A recent improvement is Crown Court where old framed buildings have been retained and provide an entrance from the main street to the car park.

Above some shops on the north side of the High Street are good examples of mid-seventeenth-century decorative brickwork. No. 80 has two pedimented gables, and Nos. 74 and 76 are conveniently dated 1663 in one of the brick panels. The cast iron window casements, which I confess I like, both here and in most other cottages where I find them, date to about 1840.

A little more of this decorative-style brickwork is to be seen in The Square opposite the King's Arms.

The old White Hart survives, as a row of shops with living accommodation above. It is said to be the inn that Dickens had in mind for Nicholas Nickleby's stop on his way to Portsmouth. Opposite the White Hart, and now as much identified with Godalming as the Guildhall clock is with Guildford, is the little Town Hall, known affectionately as the Pepper Pot.

Behind this in Church Street is a timber-framed house with curved braces that form a pattern of circles. The date of the building is probably around 1600. Next door is a house set 'end on' to the street. This indicates the increasing value of frontage in a town that was gaining importance, when houses could no longer be economically placed lengthways to the street. At Godalming this probably happened in the seventeenth century, 150 years later than in Guildford.

The parish church of Godalming, with its elegant, thirteenth-century spire well deserves its superb site. A little pre-Conquest work survives in the church: just two blocked double splayed circular windows in the west wall of the tower. Norman work remains in the east tower arch and the chancel where three blocked windows may be seen on both sides, some with painted decoration.

The Portsmouth Road left Godalming by Ockford Road, that lead to Milford where the most notable house is Milford House, built in the early decades of the eighteenth century in a heavy-handed Baroque style. Inside there is a good staircase with turned fluted balusters, typical of the early eighteenth century.

The farmhouse now known as Old Hurst is a large framed house with some stone fronting. It is of several builds with good early eighteenth-century panelling in the ground-floor rooms of the two jettied crosswings.

Apart from the A3, two other roads radiate out from Milford—one goes to Chiddingfold and the other to Haslemere.

The Chiddingfold road passes through Witley where Step Cottages, near the church, form, with the church tower and spire, one of the country's well known groupings. Although now particularly identified with this part of Surrey, tile-hanging such as that on Step Cottages, is a

relatively late feature. Its use dates from the seventeenth century.

Opposite Step Cottages, is the White Hart, part of which dates to the early fifteenth century. It is an exceptionally picturesque building and is popular for its association with George Eliot, the novelist.

Witley is a place of pilgrimage for me because the watercolour painter, Myles Birket Foster, is buried there in the churchyard. The church has eleventh-century

*Step Cottages and the church tower at Witley combine to make a picture wholly typical of Surrey*

Saxon origins in the nave where there is a Saxon double-splayed window-opening in the south wall, and another in the west gable.

A return to the Portsmouth Road can be made through the lanes via Sandhills and Brook, reaching the main road near the Half Moon and the village of Thursley. There, a lane snakes up to the church between a handful of cottages.

As at Witley, there is Saxon work in the church there. Two excellent Saxon windows can be seen in the chancel that show the typical double-splay and still have mid-wall window boards. These windows were found in 1927 and belonged to the pre-Conquest church which, together with the other work, went in the two harsh restorations of 1860 and 1883.

One other feature of importance remains, however, and this is the massive timber construction that supports the belfry. It appears to be late fifteenth-century work and is an elaborate frame of posts and braces very similar to others at Alfold and Dunsfold. The font is pre-Conquest.

West of the church is Hill Farm, a large timber-framed house which once had a two-bay open hall with arch-braced roof truss over the centre. It underwent changes and additions around 1600 when a floor was inserted in the hall and two crosswings were added. It is an excellent example of how the appearance of an old house can be changed to keep up with fashion: a brick front was built sometime after 1710 but the new front was not a perfect fit as a principal post of the old house passes in front of one of the windows.

Opposite Hill Farm is a range of buildings including one very good barn of the later sixteenth century.

Sir Edwin Lutyens grew up in Thursley at what is now Street House, and The Corner is one of his very early conversions. With his formative years spent in Thursley and the surrounding villages one does not have far to seek for the influences that formed his career.

From the slopes of Gibbet Hill, a stream flows northwards to join the River Wey at Oxenford. Along its course there is a string of lakes, one of which fed Cosford Mill. A framed house of the late sixteenth or early seventeenth century, this was shortened and, later, seventeenth century work was added. This was again added to in the eighteenth and nineteenth century. The building of Cosford Mill, therefore, covers a considerable period, but there does not appear to be actual structural evidence that any part of the present building was a mill before the mid- to late-seventeenth century.

The present owner salvaged the mill after it had become derelict and overgrown, and has restored the greater part of the machinery, although the wheel has gone.

Near Cosford Mill the main road climbs up to take a broad sweep around the Devil's Punch Bowl. Why the devil should be credited with so beautiful a place I cannot

*Hill Farm, Thursley, is a classic example of refronting an old framed house with Georgian brick*

imagine, but it is certainly like a vast bowl, or oversized Greek theatre, completely enclosed on three sides with the northern end open to give views across Surrey towards the Hog's Back and beyond.

A trackway leads round the western edge of the rim near Gibbet Hill, and along here is a commemorative stone that records the murder of a sailor on 24 September 1786 by three fellow travellers after he had befriended them and shared his money with them. The three were soon caught and hanged.

*Cosford Mill was saved from dereliction in recent years and much of the machinery survives*

# CHAPTER ELEVEN

# The Heathland Villages of North-West Surrey

The A30 London to Southampton road enters Surrey at Staines and cuts across the north-western edge of the county. Southwards, between it and the Hog's Back, is enclosed an area composed largely of open heathland, part of which is used by the military. Barracks are at St John's, Woking; Bisley; Pirbright and Deepcut near Frimley.

A road runs from Guildford to Bagshot and there are linking roads between the villages, many developed from former tracks across the heaths. To explore the area one has to follow these minor roads and lanes, taking a circular journey around the large sweeps of heather and pines on Chobham Common and the commons between Pirbright and Bagshot.

At the northern end of the A30 near Egham, there are the Royal Holloway College and Holloway Sanatorium. These two extraordinary buildings, designed by W.H. Crossland for Thomas Holloway, were a great philanthropic gesture made possible by the fortune amassed from the enormous sales of Holloway's pills and ointments. Both buildings are derivative, both examples of the heights that the ambitions of late Victorian architects could aspire to and reach.

The sanatorium was founded in 1873 and opened in 1885. Its style has been attributed to Belgian Gothic, and it has a tall, central tower rising behind a first-floor hall block with an open, arcaded ground floor. Long wings extend to each side.

The college, near Englefield Green, is in rosy red brick with stone dressings—an attractive colour scheme—inspired by the French Renaissance château of Chambord. The size of the building is staggering: it is arranged around two courtyards with grouped turreted towers at the four corners, and tower blocks on the four long sides. Such overlarge buildings of the nineteenth century are too often insipid, the architect's inspiration being overstretched, but the impression here is one of richness. The detailing is nowhere inadequate, but is used appropriately in the spirit of the French model.

Englefield Green is to the north of the A30 with the weather-boarded Barley Mow pub on the south side of the large green, and a few eighteenth- and nineteenth-century houses on the east and north sides.

The Old House has a plain brick front of about 1715 with roof and dormers showing behind a parapet. The window openings are oddly treated with Tudor dripstone

*Roman ruins from North Africa, transported to a site on a Roman road at Virginia Water, could confound future scholars*

arches—this little quirk of design is amusing—but the front porch, which looks relatively modern, spoils what is otherwise a charming façade. A Nash-type early nineteenth-century stuccoed villa with wide eaves cornice and curved end bays is nearby, and there is another similar house nearby in Clarence Drive.

Nearer the A30 the village comprises small nineteenth-century villas and terraces, many now turned into shops. Here is also a disconcerting building, the church of St Simon and St Jude, built in 1859. Brick and stone have been used for the interior walls which, with a dark brown, unvarnished pine, arch-braced roof, give a claustrophobic effect. However, the sombre interior has been enhanced by the clever choice of blue hangings and cushions for the seating, which is the original long benches.

Englefield Green stands on the borders of Windsor Great Park, and south of the village is Virginia Water, a large, ornamental lake which is best approached from the entrance near the Wheatsheaf Hotel on the A30.

In 1746 'Billy the Butcher of Culloden', Duke of Cumberland, son of George II, was made Ranger of Windsor Great Park. Between 1748 and 1757 he used the services of Thomas Sandby—brother of Paul Sandby and both now best remembered for their watercolours—in the landscaping at Virginia Water. Thomas was employed by the duke as a draughtsman and produced plans and perspective drawings for him (his drawings of the Battle of Culloden are in the Royal Collection).

Virginia Water was later enjoyed by George IV who employed Wyattville—then at work on remodelling Windsor Castle—to construct various pavilions there for him, in particular the ruin at the lakeside. This was done in 1827 with Roman columns that had lain at the British Museum since their importation in 1818 from Leptis Magna in Libya. It is amusing to think that at some period in the distant future archaeologists might find these ruins and associate them with the Roman Road—the Devil's Highway—that connected London with Silchester and the West. From Staines the road passed near the Wheatsheaf Hotel, and Virginia Water lake, to Bagshot Park where it changed direction to run almost due west out of the county.

The countryside west of the Great Park is exploited for gravel and scarred by the M3 not far away, but some rural corners remain and grandiose attempts are being made to adapt the gravel pit lakes for leisure purposes.

At Thorpe a surprising amount of the old village survives, and now that it is a conservation area, it might continue to do so—at least for a time. There are one or two framed cottages, in particular The Cottage, Village Road, which is a good example of one build placed beside another with two principal uprights side by side on the front. Near the church are several eighteenth-century

*Redlands Farm which has a superb sixteenth-century crosswing with high quality work on the joists of the parlour ceiling*

brick houses, including the handsome Thorpe House (c. 1750) and a late thatched cottage that provides a rural touch.

Thorpe was given to the abbey of Chertsey in the seventh century and remained its property until it went to Bisham Abbey near Marlow in 1537, and then to the Crown in 1538.

The semicircular chancel arch in the church is twelfth-century Norman and it alone survived the rebuilding of the church in the fourteenth century. On either side of the arch are fifteenth-century squints which would have been associated with side chapels, and in the chancel there is fourteenth-century tracery in windows of outstanding quality believed to have been the work of Chertsey Abbey masons.

Near Thorpe is the mansion of Great Fosters, dated 1598, and a typical late Elizabethan brick house with a five-gable front and central entrance.

Lyne is in the fields near the M3, and in Lyne Lane is Redlands Farm, an exceptionally interesting early hall house with an added jettied sixteenth-century crosswing in which the joists of the ground-floor parlour ceiling are beautifully finished with chamfers.

By threading through the lanes, the large complex of Botleys Park and St Peter's Hospitals is reached. The Palladian mansion of Botleys Park was built for Sir Joseph Mawbey in 1765 by Kenton Couse known locally as surveyor of the Surrey side of Chertsey Bridge and assistant to James Paine in the building of Richmond Bridge in 1774. Along with other work in London, he refronted No. 10 Downing Street and is said to have made designs for the tower of St Margaret's, Westminster, in 1735–7—an early essay in the Gothic Revival.

From Botleys the wooded lanes wind through fields as they approach Chobham and tucked amid trees are many houses of interest, in particular, Stanners Hill Farm. This was a large hall house, both ends of which have now gone, one having been replaced by a sixteenth-century crosswing.

In Chobham village the tower of the church completely dominates the High Street, a really handsome street, with the White Hart near the church, and a row of houses and shops opposite that include sixteenth- and seventeenth-century buildings, among them The Sun.

Chobham Church illustrates the poverty of good building stone in Surrey—especially in these northern parts. A variety of stone has been used, including clunch for the door and window openings, heathstone, Horsham roofing slabs and most noticeable of all, resort has been made to an extensive use of puddingstone a natural conglomerate of gravel and pebbles coloured dark plum pudding brown by the presence of iron. The south aisle wall has a chequered pattern of this material and heathstone, and the fifteenth-century tower is entirely of heathstone and has a lead spire. The original nave was eleventh century as the splayed Norman windows, cut through by a late twelfth-century south arcade, indicate.

From Chobham to Horsell the lanes go past the R.S.P.C.A. Millbrook Centre where stray animals are taken from a wide area and cared for until they can be found new homes. The buildings of the centre are laid out in pleasant fields, and the annual open day is becoming a popular and well-attended event to which many local dogs are happy to take their owners!

*Botleys Park belongs to a late Palladian phase in England and externally is more attractive than Clandon Park*

*The Mosque at Woking, still used as a place of worship*

Horsell is very much a heathland village. Indeed, Horsell Common still borders it, and may continue to do so as long as Horsell Common Preservation Society can exist on subscriptions from only a fraction of the people who benefit from its endeavours.

A small, but very good example of a sixteenth-century hall house is in Cheapside. The cottage has now been restored and shows a process of development in which a hall house has been 'floored' and a smoke bay made; then, finally, a brick chimney has been placed in the smoke bay.

Horsell Church is well sited, standing at the edge of the roadway on Church Hill. Thoroughly restored by W.F. Unsworth and with its fifteenth-century tower, it is still visually a great asset to the village.

Across Horsell Common, near the Basingstoke Canal, is a disused Moslem burial ground with gateway and surrounding wall. It has been suggested—but I do not know with how much truth—that Lutyens had a hand in the design of it in 1916.

This cemetery was associated with the nearby mosque in Oriental Road, built in 1889 for the Oriental University Institute. The institute had been opened by Dr Gottlieb Wilhelm Leitner in a building that was formerly The Royal Dramatic College, a retreat for aged actors and actresses. There were great hopes for the success of both these ventures, but both failed in turn and now a fragment of the old building may be seen in the Lion Works complex—a first-floor hall and a cloister with carvings depicting characters from Shakespeare.

North-west from the Lion Works across Horsell Common (where, at the sandpit, H.G. Wells set the opening of *The War of the Worlds*) is Littlewick Road which leads to Knaphill. At the approach to Anchor Hill, at the corner of Barrs Lane is Inwood, a large framed house with two later crosswings.

The original house had a smoke bay and is probably of mid-sixteenth-century date. A large chimney was put in the smoke bay and a chamber seems to have existed outside this brick stack—but within the roof space—for smoking hams.

In a lane off Anchor Hill is The Barley Mow, a seventeenth-century house with some framing at the rear. Not far away, across the fields, is Bisley Church which, unfortunately, has been restored. However, the framework supporting the shingled belfry is of great interest and has been dated as fourteenth century. It does not stand independently as do those at Alfold and Thursley, but is tied to the nave walls by moulded beams.

There is a simple Jacobean pulpit, and at the west tower entrance a handsome, fourteenth-century timber porch with massive principal corner posts of great width which are shaped to form an arch—the extravagant use of timber here is worthy of Warwickshire.

In Clews Lane, near the church, is Clews Farm, a large sixteenth-century farmhouse which is one of the best houses in the district.

From Bisley the main road to Guildford leads down to Brookwood and the cemetery. This is part of the land around Woking which was purchased by the London Necropolis and National Mausoleum Company for the "interment of the dead of the Metropolis and suburbs beyond the boundaries".

Pirbright is to the west of Brookwood Cemetery and is a small village with a large green complete with pond.

*Pirbright Church has a fine tower built of sarsens, with galleted mortar joints*

*Merrist Wood, Worplesdon, one of Norman Shaw's most likeable houses, but sadly, severely damaged by fire in 1978*

There are no really outstanding houses here, but to compensate there is the most delightful grouping of buildings of various periods. Even the village hall on the green, erected as late as 1901, is an asset, and the charming little statue of a girl nearby is an added bonus.

In Mill Lane, beyond the green, is a pretty, late eighteenth-century Mill House near a stream. Beyond Mill House is Pirbright Lodge, built in 1774 by Vice-Admiral the Honourable John Byron, grandfather of the poet. The older work may be evident within, but the stuccoed front looks early nineteenth century with its rounded ends and verandas reminiscent of Nash.

Pirbright Parish Church stands away from the green to the west. The tower is of local sarsen or heathstone, galleted with ironstone—small pieces of stone pushed into the mortar to prevent erosion. In 1784 the nave and a chancel were built in brick with a north arcade of Doric columns and a gallery (part of the gallery was removed in 1973). The present east end is a replacement of 1848.

The nave is a good example of brickwork with the use of red rubbers for the window arches and red and blue-grey header bond for the walling. The windows are repeated on the north side, but economies were made on the walling which is in Flemish bond.

Finally, north of the church is Wickham Farm, a large, framed structure with two added crosswings.

From Pirbright the Guildford road runs through Worplesdon, past Rickford Mill, now a private house, then Norton Farm, a seventeenth-century framed building, up to the village where there is a green that is small, at least by Surrey standards. An interesting example of the early refronting, in the late seventeenth century, of a timber-framed house faces the green, and nearby is a late sixteenth-century barn, once the village smithy and probably doomed to demolition in the near future.

Hollow Trees, nearby, is a house of several periods, and in part much restored, but it has a delightful brick cross-wing, dated in the gable but difficult to decipher. It is about 1720.

Norman Shaw did a considerable amount of work in Surrey, and Merrist Wood at Worplesdon was, I think, one of his best houses. Regrettably it has been seriously damaged by fire and the crownpost first-floor hall has been lost.

The house had the three features always present in Shaw's designs: a massive entrance porch, a large oriel window lighting the hall and at least one large spectacular chimney-stack. Merrist Wood had these features and perhaps more successfully than in his other houses it shows Shaw's love of massive scale to obtain dramatic effect kept under control. The house is now part of a complex of later buildings and is used as an agricultural college.

Near the Worplesdon gate to Merrist Wood is Perry Hill Farm, built about 1560 as a house with a single bay hall. (It is datable from the use of reducing principal rafters). When an upper floor was inserted in the hall a smoke bay was made in the service bay. To this a lower extension was added to compensate for the space thus lost. Later this extension was increased in height to conform with the line of the main roof. The smoke bay conversion was, perhaps, undertaken in 1600–10 and a brick chimney was put in the smoke bay later—about 1640–50.

Southwards along the road to Guildford is Pitch Place where there is a later seventeenth-century brick house with Dutch, pedimented, gables. Houses in this style are always attractive both for their colour and for the quality of the brickwork.

Not far from Pitch Place along Gravetts Lane, is the handsome brick Frosbury farmhouse which might have early work at the rear. Then near Aldershot Road, at the edge of Broadstreet Common, is Whites Farm, where an old friend once lived. It is dated 1670 in the brickwork of the two-storey porch and has a perfect example of a mid-seventeenth-century roof in pristine condition with butted purlins not in line.

On warm summer days I have sat in the garden of this house, and well-plied with good home-brewed ale, I have listened to gentle conversation punctuated by the hum of bees and the song of birds in the garden and on the common beyond.

At Wood Street Green is Billhurst Farm, a fine early eighteenth-century house well sited near the village pond. Also at Wood Street is Comptons Farm, once a hall house but now notable for its very good seventeenth-century crosswing.

North of Wood Street is Littlefield Manor which has a brick front later than the house at Pitch Place, about 1700, and therefore anticipating eighteenth-century elegance with more assurance. At the rear the house is timber framed.

Along the Aldershot Road from Littlefield Common is Whipley Farm, now a large house, but its first build was a small framed house of about 1550. A larger house of two bays and a stack was added to this about 1625 and was followed by a dated crosswing of 1735.

Across the fields from Whipley is Passengers Farm which is in Worplesdon parish, but near Normandy and within sight of the ridge of the Hog's Back to the south. This farmhouse is still part of a working farm and the original building was almost certainly a small two-bay open hall house of the early sixteenth century. To this a smokebay and two further bays were added in the later sixteenth century. A brick chimney was subsequently built in the smokebay in the seventeenth century.

At Normandy there is Longerend Cottage, a sixteenth-century house built around a central brick chimney. The house has been carefully preserved and extended; apart from other original details there are a few

*Whites Farm, Worplesdon, is typical of the unassuming, simple beauty of the many farmhouses that are scattered through the Surrey countryside*

*The tower of Ash Church, seen behind Hartshorn Cottage, once an inn known as The Whitehart and probably dating to the mid-sixteenth century*

of the old 'solid' triangular section type treads remaining in the stair beside the chimney. Glaziers is interesting and proved difficult to identify until it was realized that it was a barn conversion of many years standing.

In contrast to these smaller houses is Westwood House with an eighteenth-century façade but with a tiny sixteenth-century timber-framed wing.

The fifteenth-century heathstone tower and Victorian shingled spire of Ash Church is a landmark in this area, and very beautiful it can be, especially when seen in the panoramic views from the Hog's Back. The church was thoroughly restored in 1865, and has some fascinating and elaborate nineteenth-century roof structures.

West of the church, towards Aldershot, is Merryworth, an attractive late framed house recently restored. It is officially listed as 1510, which is obviously inaccurate, it being some 100 years later at least. There is a large brick stack with good original brick arches to some of the fireplaces. Much close studding is evident, both externally at the end facing the road and inside. The main roof is of seventeenth-century butted purlin type.

At Ash Wharf can be seen the Basingstoke Canal—much effort is being expended to restore it to its past glory.

It follows the road through Ash Vale and Mytchett to Frimley Green where there is still a pleasant open green. The area has mostly Victorian and later development, but a few ancient houses are near the green, especially the late sixteenth-century Bedfords Farm and its thatched barn now prettily converted as a dwelling.

In Cross Lane is Cross Farm, timber-framed and late fifteenth century but with many later additions, including a jettied end that, if original, is much restored. Almost opposite is Cross Cottage which has a framed section once hung with slate and, at right angles to it, a brick wing that looks like seventeenth-century work, although the house is officially dated as 1713.

To conclude, we move north-east through Bagshot to Windlesham. The church here was damaged by fire in 1680 and was rebuilt in brick. Then, in the nineteenth century, a chancel and nave were added so that of the original work there now remains only a little seventeenth-century brickwork on the south side including the brick porch.

Near the church is The Cedars built about 1720, and in Pound Lane there are the two sixteenth-century houses, Pound Meadow and the thatched Pound Cottage, almost certainly built with a centre smoke bay.

*Stanwell Church has very fine fifteenth-century blank arcading in the chancel*

# CHAPTER TWELVE

# The River Thames

Runnymede will for ever be enshrined in the minds of free men as the place where the precious liberties upon which freedom depends were laid down by the signing of the Magna Carta on a June day in 1215.

These liberties have been jealously guarded throughout history, but at no time were they more at peril than during the last war when thousands of young men of many nationalities died for those ideals.

For those who fought in the air there could be no more fitting place for a memorial than the heights above Runnymede. A place so elevated it might be suspended in the sky.

The Air Forces Memorial was designed by Sir Edward Maufe. The entrance to the building is surmounted by an eagle sculpture by Esmond Burton and leads directly to the cloisters, where are recorded the names of 20,455 north and west Europe based Commonwealth Air Forces personnel who died over North-West Europe and the West-ern Approaches and who have no known grave. These names are carved on tablets of Derbyshire marble which are so arranged in pairs, vertically and at an angle, that they simulate the appearance of open books. Each pair thus forms a niche.

Opposite the entrance, across the cloister lawns at the centre of which is a stone of Remembrance, is a tall tower. In outline this tower appropriately appears to symbolize an airfield control tower: it has a single, large arch, above which are bas-reliefs representing Justice, Victory and Courage. Within, it has a high vaulted chamber or shrine that has a large window on which is engraved two winged figures holding a scroll inscribed with the 139th Psalm.

The architectural treatment of this building is, I think, deliberately simple, almost unassuming. It is rather like any of the hundreds of little known, unpretentious mountain monasteries in Italy and Greece, it is there for a purpose beyond values limited by architectural merit alone. Fitting architecture is needed for such a memorial but in the final count it is the silent presence of those 20,455 names that matters.

Downstream from Runnymede is Staines Bridge, built by Sir John Rennie between 1829 and 1832. It leads to Clarence Street where a little character yet remains in the much-altered George IV terraced buildings on the north side. Eastwards, where Church Street and Clarence Street meet the High Street, is the Blue Anchor, an inn of the early eighteenth century with vitrified header bricks used with red ones to make a chequered pattern. At the side of the inn a small framed structure of the seventeenth century is now contained in later work.

The parish church of St Mary is away from the centre of the town at the end of Church Street in a quiet backwater where much development and restoration is taking place. The church was rebuilt in 1828 by J.B. Watson and includes window tracery and an interior balcony in cast iron. Further work was done in 1885 when the apse and chancel roof were added. A tablet in the tower records that it was built by Inigo Jones in 1631. Be that as it may, it is a good tower in liver-coloured brick. The upper section was reconstructed in 1828.

Northwards out of Staines a road passes between the high embankments of the King George VI and Staines reservoirs to Stanwell, Poyle and Colnbrook once part of Middlesex.

At Colnbrook the old Ostrich Inn is now the most impressive building in the village and is a long, continuous jetty house with gabled wings at each end that are also jettied.

The village of Stanwell is dominated by the fine church that stands to the south of a small triangular green. Fortunately, the church has escaped extensive restoration: only the north aisle was rebuilt by S.S. Teulon in 1863 and the south aisle and the nave have been re-roofed above the old tiebeams and wallplates. The nave arcade is thirteenth century with a fifteenth-century clerestory. The chancel has a considerable amount of fifteenth-century blank arcading on both the north and south sides and these have cusped ogee arches with Purbeck marble shafts, bases and capitals. A shaft piscina of the twelfth century has been discovered in the chancel.

The chancel is further enriched by a superb example of seventeenth-century carving in a beautiful state of preservation—the tomb of Thomas, Lord Knyvett, and his wife (1622) by Nicolas Stone.

Around the village green are one or two pleasant eighteenth- and nineteenth-century houses, particularly Dunmore House.

Besides being commemorated in the church, Lord Knyvett and his wife are remembered for the free school, founded in their name in 1624 and standing a little to the east of the village. The interior is divided into a large schoolroom extending to the full height of the building and entered by the left-hand front door. The right-hand side was the master's house with first-floor and attic rooms.

At Ashford there is now a good shopping centre—and a well-stocked library.

Southwards out of Ashford is Laleham, a small group of buildings including some eighteenth- and nineteenth-century houses around a church and near the river.

Dial House, on the main road south of the church, has the date and initials 1730HW on a sundial, but the Doric portico of the front entrance and bay windows are later. Church Farm, to the east of the church is late seventeenth century and the large stuccoed High Elms and The Limes, on the curve at the start of Blacksmith's Lane opposite the church, complete the group.

Laleham Church has a rather ponderous brick tower of 1732 but there is Tudor brickwork in the north chancel chapel. Inside there is a Norman south and north arcade with large cylindrical columns and scalloped capitals—the south arcade was blocked when the south aisle was removed long ago. In the churchyard are the graves of Matthew Arnold, his wife, their sons and their grandsons.

From Laleham, downstream beyond the M3 bridge, is Chertsey Bridge. Dickens described this location in *Oliver Twist* and gave an accurate account of it at that time, about 1837. The old house by the bridge, "ruinous and decayed" where Sikes and Oliver rested for a while, has gone, but it stood there until about 1850. It was the Black Swan, and was last occupied by a Mr Rostwell. It stood on what was the Middlesex bank, downstream of the bridge.

Dickens did not describe the actual bridge, but he would have known it, as it was built in 1787. Chertsey Bridge is an architect's bridge designed in a specific 'style'.

Perhaps in bridges, more than any other form of architecture, the great gulf between attitudes medieval and modern (in the broadest sense) can be most easily seen. A medieval bridge was always built to suit the particular crossing. Its arches varied in width—and thus height—to accommodate the volume of water flowing through them. So the greater arches would not necessarily be at the centre, but nearer to one bank than the other as the river dictated, and this determined the curve of the bridge. Therefore, by yielding to the natural forces of the water in its design, a man-made structure was at once practical and in harmony with its surroundings.

Westwards from the bridge a road leads into the town—the route taken by Sikes and Oliver on their way, perhaps, to Pyrcroft; the house on the south-western margin of the town that is romantically connected with Dickens's story.

In medieval times the wealthy and powerful abbey of Chertsey stood in the water-meadows a little to the north of the present church. At the Dissolution Henry VIII expended his anger upon it by ensuring its swift and vicious destruction. Practically no trace of the abbey remains above ground; all that survives is a stone arch—said to be thirteenth century—in a hedge in Colonel's Lane.

Unfortunately, no buildings of pre-Dissolution date—except parts of the church and perhaps the little George Inn in Guildford Street—appear to remain in the town either. Indeed, there is also little of the late sixteenth or

*Chertsey Bridge, one of the finest bridges over the Thames but it could be in danger of damage by modern traffic*

seventeenth century. The jettied houses, Nos. 44–48, London Street, could be early sixteenth century, but they have been altered, refaced in eighteenth-century brick and given a pediment. Chertsey today dates mainly from the eighteenth century onwards although its houses and shops may line the old roads that led to the abbey and now meet at the church, the focal point of the town.

The tower of the parish church of Chertsey is medieval except for the upper part, and is built in a pleasant mixture of materials. Other old work remains: there is a fifteenth-century chancel arch and two medieval arches on the south side of the chancel, and there is a crownpost roof also in the chancel. However, for the most part the building fell victim to a very unsympathetic restoration in 1806–8. A curfew bell is still rung from the tower every evening from Michaelmas to Lady Day.

In London Street is the Town Hall (1851), a good building of its kind, Italianate, of Palladian, not Gothic, ancestry. It has to compete with the heavy timbered effect of The Crown on one side, but on the other there is a pleasant row of stuccoed houses of about 1830.

Guildford Street, the main shopping street, has one or two notable buildings, although modern shop-fronts have spoilt them. At the southern end is the George Inn—small, timber-framed and fifteenth century in part—and the new public library, well-sited near a little stream and an unobtrusive, pleasant building.

Near the north end is the King's Head, a large eighteenth-century double pile, the twin roofs ending at the front in a common hip.

At No. 113 is a brick front of the mid-eighteenth century with a stone pediment surmounted by an exceptionally high disproportionate parapet.

The building in the street with the most character is undoubtedly the large Victorian polychrome brick shop

*Curfew House, Chertsey, has been attributed to one of Hawksmoor's assistants*

with large plate-glass windows. There are distant echoes of Ruskin's *Stones of Venice* in the grouping of the first-floor windows between barley-sugar twist shafts with Italian Gothic capitals.

In Windsor Street, west of the church, are the best of the town's houses. The most impressive are Nos. 8–16 including Curfew House. This block was built by Sir William Perkins to house a school he founded, and the inscription in the pediment over the centre window of Curfew House admonishes "For fifty children clothed and taught. Go and do likewise. 1725".

A contract, still extant, was drawn up in 1723 between Sir William and Edward Reeves, builder, of Twickenham. The centre portion of the house is shown in an original drawing without the present attic storey.

The Cedars, also in Windsor Street, is now the home of the Chertsey Museum. A documented history of The Cedars site, on the corner of Alwyns Lane, goes back to at least the mid-sixteenth century when an inn, The Anngell, is mentioned. This inn had ceased to exist when the property was purchased by Sir William Perkins in 1701. A newly-erected house is mentioned in 1747, but stylistically, the present house could not be this one as it appears to be early nineteenth century. However, the Little Cedars, once part of the house, is probably earlier. The roof with its wide eaves is an example of the 'engineer's' roof. It is in softwood and has kingposts in tension strapped to the tie-beams with iron plates.

The road eastwards out of Chertsey continues on the northern side of the river to Shepperton. A lane also loops from this road to run alongside the Thames down to Shepperton Lock. It is here, in a network of watercourses, that the River Wey and the Wey Navigation join the Thames. Here also is The Eyot, or D'Oyly Carte Island. The father of Rupert D'Oyly Carte hoped to use the island site as an annexe to the Savoy Hotel, but as he was unable to go ahead with the scheme, lived there himself. The place also became associated with his son's operatic work.

At Shepperton the church stands above the river at the eastern end of a small square surrounded by a cottagey group of the eighteenth century and the nineteenth century including the Old Ferry House, Thames Cottage and Ye Olde House, the two latter both having good doorcases.

The Rectory is also in the square, north of the church. It has a deceptive eighteenth-century façade, not in brick as it appears, but mathematical tiles, and this conceals a late fifteenth-century framed hall house.

The church, of flint and stone, part arranged as a chequer pattern, is early seventeenth century, and the west tower is in a good grey-brown brick and is dated 1710. Inside, early nineteenth-century fittings include a gallery at the west end with a well-painted Royal Arms, box pews, pulpit and chancel screen. The small interior and the

*The Cedars now houses the Chertsey Museum, the Little Cedars adjoining may be a fragment of an earlier house*

*The Manor House at Walton was a hall house and dates to the fifteenth century. The hall was later floored but in modern times the floor was removed although the crownpost roof is still ceiled*

appropriately small scale fittings combine to produce a particularly satisfying result.

From the square the road runs away from the Thames, then separates—one fork is Shepperton High Street, but the other returns to meet a wide loop in the river and, continuing past a large open green, leads towards Lower Halliford and Walton. Along this road are one or two good houses. First, a group including Thamesfield, Clonskeagh, Willow House and Willow Bank, a pleasant row dating from the eighteenth to the late nineteenth century.

Next comes Halliford School in a late Palladian style with brick pediment and stuccoed ground floor, now without character and not helped by the nineteenth-century renewal of all the sashes which now have single large panes. Of the hotels along this stretch, the River View Hotel, situated where the river loops up to the road, has the best view.

Then, around the large green, are a weather-boarded house with additions, and Dunally House and Dunally Lodge which form an irregular terrace block. Peacock House, nearby, was the home of Thomas Love Peacock, the poet, who lived there from 1823–66, and with whose daughter George Meredith, the poet, who lived at Box Hill, had a disastrous marriage. Battlecrease is a large late eighteenth-century house with an odd portico combining Ionic capitals with pointed arches cut into the architrave.

Returning to Shepperton, the High Street leads to the

station past uninteresting recent developments, and then beyond Shepperton Green is the road to Littleton. Once there was a very pleasant group of buildings near the film studios here, but the church is all that remains of it and further development of land south of the church will complete the sad transformation.

Littleton Church is a gem. It has a brick tower of the early sixteenth century, a brick porch and a brick clerestory. There is a north chapel of 1705 and another of 1730, both in brick. Although the early, thirteenth-century, church was in stone and flint, brick now dominates, its colour varying with the dates of the different builds from the orange-red of the clerestory to the dull grey-pink of the lower parts of the tower.

The Walton Bridge that Turner knew and painted soon after 1800 has gone, the present ugly structure being a temporary bridge replacing an unsafe iron bridge of 1859. Turner's bridge was built in 1779 by James Paine, who also built Chertsey Bridge.

Walton is now a busy shopping centre with the usual development of characterless, box-like structures, but there are several reminders of the past in the High Street, notably No. 47 which was built about 1650, and in No. 17 Church Street, Admiral Rodney is said to have been born.

In Manor Road, near the river, is the Manor House. This is one of the best houses of its kind in Surrey and has much original work. It was built as a hall house around 1450, and within a century, two crosswings had been added. The two-bay hall had a floor and ceiling inserted probably in the late sixteenth or seventeenth century, but the floor has been removed. The roof timbers, however, are still obscured by a ceiling.

The cross-passage, once entered by doors at the front and rear of the house, remains, as do the doors from the passage that once gave access to the service rooms. As was so often the case in the many changes and additions made to houses like this, the original, simple plan has been confused by the replanning of internal, domestic uses whereby the parlour and service ends are interchanged—often several times as at Vine Cottages, Shere.

Walton Church is reputed to contain Saxon stonework, but the most evident early work is the late Norman, c.1180, north nave arcade, a row of large cylindrical piers with scalloped capitals. The Norman church was rebuilt in the fourteenth century and in the sixteenth century the north aisle was raised in height by building in brick above the early stonework. If the sixteenth-century date for this is correct, it is an early use of brick in Surrey for this purpose and may be compared with similar work at Littleton and Laleham.

The nave roof was replaced about 1634 whether this was done because of the subsidence of the north arcade, or because of fire, cannot be verified but it appears that this roof is rare in that it has a date. This is important, because

*Walton Church, in which the nave roof can be dated to about 1634, an important date reference in calculating the spread southwards of innovations introduced into seventeenth-century roof construction*

it establishes the use of a particular roof structure, namely butt side purlins not in line, at a time and place in the spread of its use southwards out of London.

Walton Church is also noted for the Shannon monument by Roubiliac, erected in 1755. It is a superb, large composition in marble, depicting Viscount Shannon leaning upon a cannon and surrounded by all the paraphernalia of battle. On the plinth below is the figure of his daughter.

Sunbury is north of the Thames, the old village centre being by the river where there are a number of villas, which, when they were built, were almost at the western extremity of the development of the Thames riverside as a country retreat from London.

Orchard House has an early eighteenth century parapeted brick façade, and original gate piers and railings. Monksbridge is a little later and is set at right angles to the road so that it is not only itself set off to good advantage, but adds greatly to the interest of the street.

Sunbury Church was originally built in 1752 by a clerk of works at Hampton Court, but little of this survived a rebuild by S.S. Teulon in 1856.

East of the church is Darby House with Gothic-style windows in a large bay on the side of the houses facing the river, but a more conventional Palladian-style front entrance. Then Sunbury Court, a large red-brick house with stone dressings, pilasters and pediment in Palladian style,

now beautifully maintained by the Salvation Army.

The road from Sunbury follows the riverbank and leaves Surrey. Passing the extraordinary brick, tower-like *palazzos* of the water board, it enters Hampton where, in a garden opposite the church, there is the Garrick Temple which was once in David Garrick's garden. Beyond Hampton, the road leads to Hampton Court, and then over the bridge designed by Lutyens, to re-enter Surrey at East Molesey where the River Mole flows into the Thames.

From Hampton Court Bridge the river borders Hampton Court Park on one side and Thames Ditton on the other. Near the old Swan Inn at Thames Ditton, a small suspension bridge crosses to an island in the river, where the scene is further enhanced by the lawns and eighteenth-century façade of Boyle Farm, now the Home of Compassion.

The parish church nearby has a thirteenth-century flint and stone west tower, quaintly topped with weatherboarding and surmounted by a small needle spire. Inside the church is an unusual fifteenth-century Easter sepulchre with a canopy supported upon six arches.

The village atmosphere continues along the High Street with a variety of late eighteenth- and early nineteenth-century houses, including a canopied butcher's shop with an 1820s acanthus motif cast-iron decoration.

Then, at the junction with Station Road and Watts

Road, is a superb brick terrace of the 1740s with giant pilasters. All the original doorcases and sashes remain, only a Victorian bay at No. 1 has been added.

The Manor House nearby is a mixture of styles and the brick entrance arch is probably of the same Victorian pseudo sixteenth-century style as the ponderous garden front. Yet again, further westwards, is more brickwork, fine in its simplicity—the Henry Bridges Almshouses of 1720 which are beautifully restored and cared for.

Weston Green is part of an open space, including Sandown Park Race Course, that is crossed by the railway and the road to Hampton Court.

There are several eighteenth-century houses in the area, in particular, The Elms. At Nos. 64–66 Weston Park there is an interesting example of keeping up with the Joneses. An early seventeenth-century cottagey building was given, in the early nineteenth century, a grand new front in classical style. At a distance this gives the illusion of a solid building in brick and stucco, but on closer inspection it can be seen to be only wood and plaster which seems to lean against the older house like a piece of scenery in a Hollywood backlot. It is a most delightful building.

Returning to Watts Road we pass weather-boarded Rose Cottage and Surrey Lodge which looks a little odd with its tiled pitched roof above a classical portico. The way leads to Giggshill Green, a wide open space bordered on one side by the main road to Kingston and, on the other, by St Leonard's Cottages. There is other property, but none is so perfectly sited as this plain brick, pedimented terrace with Gothic windows.

Finally, as the main road runs into Kingston-upon-Thames, there is a pretty weather-boarded house, Fawler Cottage, Giggshill Green, almost hidden by the trees in its front garden. It looks late eighteenth century and it has a delightful doorcase. This house is quite the nicest in the immediate area.

*The Shannon Monument in Walton Parish Church is a large composition in marbles of slightly varying colours that enhance the sense of perspective created by the carving*

*The Bell Inn is a picturesque sixteenth-century inn near St Mary's Church, East Molesey*

# CHAPTER THIRTEEN

# River Mole

The River Mole enters the Thames with the River Ember after passing under a bridge designed by Sir Edwin Lutyens and just a little to the south of Hampton Court Bridge.

In Bridge Street, East Molesey, near the appropriately Tudor-style Hampton Court railway station, is a collection of interesting shops, pubs and cottagey buildings, mostly nineteenth century, but with some earlier work.

The older nucleus of East Molesey appears to be around the church of St Mary. In Bell Road, just south of the church is The Bell Inn, a picturesque house listed as *c.* 1550. It is timber-framed beneath a layer of stucco and has two large gables and one small one at the front with an upper floor gabled central porch.

Nearby is the Old Manor House. It looks seventeenth century although the Dutch-style gable on the north side of the front block appears to be restored and the doorcase and sashes are at least late nineteenth century. Quillets

Royal, adjoining, shows a little framing at the front and its earliest parts could be sixteenth century.

The village atmosphere in Bell Road is enhanced by terraces of early nineteenth-century houses. On one side of the street the front doors open on to the pavement and on the other there are front gardens. The latter are in dull yellow stock brick under a pantile roof, while the other, longer terrace has been colour-washed by individual occupiers with pleasing effect.

At West Molesey there is a small church with a nice late Gothic west tower of stone with a prominent stair turret. The rest of the church is in yellow brick built in the mid-nineteenth century and it makes a little oasis in an otherwise architecturally bleak area.

From the Sandown Park area the River Mole continues across open land without restrictions and confinement of urbanized embankments. Indeed, this most fortunate stream suffers little such interference except for a stretch just short of a mile in length where it is forced into a union with the River Ember.

The Mole passes to the west of Waynflete's Tower at Esher. To the east is Waylands Farm—a gabled brick house of about 1650 standing on a moated site.

Whiteley village, west of the river and off Seven Hills Road, was built with money left for the purpose by William Whiteley of Whiteley's Stores. The ground was purchased in 1911 and building took place from 1914–21. The

*Ham Manor, Cobham, an early eighteenth-century house with a front that retains original features. The first-floor sashes are, however, a later alteration*

village was for "thrifty old people" and was designed on a concentric plan with roads radiating from a central green where there was a statue by Sir George Frampton, R.A. The church is in a Gothic style, but this was avoided for the rest of the work. A more Baroque style was chosen for the chapel and focal points in the layout are formed by using cupolas on some of the houses in the north-south avenue.

The river flows to the west of Pains Hill Park and in a wide curve before reaching the busy village of Cobham. Surrey has its fair share of particularly picturesque arrangements where landscape and buildings are related in a way that seems almost contrived. Such a grouping is at Cobham where the roadway borders the river and the scene includes the old mill and a group of houses including the eighteenth-century Cedars and Ham Manor. The front of Cedars is probably a little later than Ham Manor, but at the rear it has a timber-framed hall house with a large re-used traceried window.

Cobham Church was a simple, aisle-less church with a north chapel opening out of the chancel through a two-bay arcade. Several disastrous restorations—probably four—have left only a Norman south doorway and a Norman tower in carstone and flint.

Bordering the churchyard is Church Stile House, an impressive building which has a double jetty and looks mid-seventeenth century. To the south of the church is a small group; Churchgate House, tile-hung and early eighteenth century, also a small cottage with ogee windows in the Gothic style.

Upstream from Cobham the river flows past open agricultural land near Cobham Tilt, Downside, Stoke D'Abernon, Slyfield, Pachesham and then Leatherhead.

At Cobham Tilt, Ashford Farm House has a brick front of about 1650 with cornice and pilasters, while at the rear there is some timber framing.

Downside is a mainly nineteenth-century group of buildings around a large green. Downside Farm is exceptionally attractive with a small range of farm buildings, not particularly old but well grouped on rising ground.

Stoke D'Abernon Church is well known for its very fine brasses of Sir John D'Abernon (1277) and his son, Sir John (1327). It cannot be denied that the church was badly restored in 1866 and much valuable work was lost. However, there are still remains to indicate that there was a pre-Conquest church on the site. These include part of an apse exposed in the north chapel, also a doorway high up in the Saxon south wall. It is conjectured that this entrance gave access to an upper chamber in the Saxon nave, a feature which was not unusual at this period. In the twelfth century a Norman north aisle was added and thirteenth-century stone vaulting was inserted in the chancel.

To the north of the chancel is the Norbury Chapel, probably built by Sir John Norbury in the reign of Henry

*Stoke D'Abernon Church, where much of interest remains in one of Surrey's oldest, and also most heavily restored, churches*

*One of the small cottages at Pachesham, built as an end smoke-bay house in the later sixteenth century, it has had considerable additions in recent years*

VII as a thanksgiving after Bosworth Field, Sir John died in 1521 and his monument, which stood in the chapel, was "by injury of time demolisht". He is now commemorated by a small kneeling figure in armour of Charles I's time.

Southwards from Stoke D'Abernon is Slyfield Manor, a large seventeenth-century brick house that incorporates fragments of a much earlier late fifteenth- or sixteenth-century courtyard house. The present building has a giant order of pilasters with Ionic volutes.

A large Dutch gabled wing is to the left of the front, and inside it is a panelled upper room with a barrel-shaped plaster ceiling which has swags, cherubs and birds. This has been dated to *c.* 1625 and other ceilings in the house, although simpler, are of *c.* 1640.

The staircase, built about 1640, is the finest of its period in the county and has carved open work panels and rusticated newel posts.

To the north of the main house is Slyfield Farm which is part of the service wings of the courtyard house complex, but, like the main block, it is clothed in mid-seventeenth-century brickwork. Inside, however, the timber-framing can be clearly seen, and it reveals that the service wings were galleried—as was the range of lodgings at Farnham Castle. The original roof does not remain on the main block, where there is a butted side purlin construction contemporary with the brickwork, on the service wings there is a crownpost roof of a type used in the late fifteenth century.

Above Slyfield the Mole meanders through farmland near Pachesham where there are two framed cottages of the later sixteenth century, at least one of which was built with an end smoke bay. Both cottages have been restored recently and the one with the smoke bay now has a large extension. The Mole flows beneath Leatherhead Bridge where there has been a crossing since ancient times. Originally there was a ford, but a bridge was built for use when the river was in flood. It is on record that in 1362 a licence was granted to collect money for the repair of a bridge.

In 1782 an Act was passed making the bridge county property and providing for its widening. It was at this time that the present fourteen-arch bridge with stone piers and brick parapet was built by George Gwilt.

At the foot of the bridge, before the road climbs up to the town, is The Running Horse, partly fifteenth century, but with later alterations and additions. The inn is associated with Skelton, the poet laureate of Henry VIII, who wrote a poem *The Tunnynge of Elynoure Rummynge*. In a 1571 edition of his work is a crude woodcut of Elynoure shown as an ill-favoured hag and her ale seems to have resulted in some riotous behaviour.

From Leatherhead the Mole flows towards Dorking through a gap in the Downs and passes a steep escarpment to the east. This is Box Hill, a popular place of resort at least since the late seventeenth century, as is clear from contemporary writings. Aubrey in his *Surrey* (1718), says that "The great quantity and thickness of the box wood yielded a convenient Privacy for Lovers". Defoe, writing at the end of the seventeenth century in his *Tour* refers to Box Hill as "A place of resort for the gentry taking the waters at Epsom".

Various writers, including Defoe, have noted the swallow-holes along the Mole. Defoe remarks that the river did "sink insensibly away". The swallows are subterranean holes or clefts in the chalk, some in the river bed, others in the banks, and it has been reported that in summer the river has been known to become a dry bed with stagnant pools. The name of the river is popularly believed to have derived from its disappearance underground like a mole.

Before road improvements in 1755, the road through the valley to Dorking was impassable for wheeled traffic in bad weather. However, as I intend to trace the route of the Roman Stane Street in my final chapter I will omit

*Leatherhead Bridge of fourteen arches was built in 1782 by George Gwilt and widened on the south side in 1824, this side is shown in the drawing*

mention of the roadway and Mickleham at this time.

From Leatherhead to Dorking the Mole is part of a most idyllic landscape. I cannot visit it without recalling most vividly John Brett's picture *The Stonebreaker* at the Walker Art Gallery, Liverpool, in which he has shown a youth breaking flints set against a background of the Mole valley with Box Hill in the distance. Truly Ruskin said of the picture, "We have here by the help of art the power of visiting a place. . . ."

I like to be near Box Hill most especially in the early summer when, oddly, the memory of this particular picture, by its art, assists me to look at the scene and be more strongly aware of the brilliancy and clarity of the colour, together with that particularly milky blue distance of chalk downland.

There is also, on such early summer days, a heightened awareness of detail, of a Pre-Raphaelite kind, from the insect on a daisy at one's feet to the clearly defined individual clumps of box tree bushes on the slopes of Box Hill.

There is a pathway across the valley through Norbury Park and from it the view in Brett's picture can still be seen almost unchanged. Up here, along a private driveway, is the mansion of Norbury Park, a house built in 1774 by Thomas Sandby for William Lane.

On the garden side is a central ground floor room with a large bay window that overlooks the valley towards Dorking. The entire walls of this room are covered with landscape views painted by George Barrett, and there is a painted ceiling by Pastorini and Cipriani.

South of Norbury Park the Mole is crossed by the roadway at Burford Bridge where it passes at the foot of Box Hill. Then, at Pixham where it bypasses Dorking, it receives the little Pippbrook Stream which once powered Pixham Mill. This mill, now no longer working, is of late date, but it combines with the seventeenth-century framed Mill House to make a delightful group.

From Pixham a footpath follows the mill stream of Castle Mill and leads to Castle Mill itself and the Mill House. Both these buildings are early nineteenth century and make a perfect pair.

The Mill House is a simple brick building, virtually unchanged since it was built: it still has a porticoed front entrance and original sash-windows and shutters.

The mill is large, 'L' shaped and weather-boarded; it came to the end of its working life in the 1950s but has been restored and adapted as a private residence.

The name of this mill is derived from the nearby Betchworth Castle, now a ruin on a bank above the Mole. It was fortified in the fourteenth and fifteenth century but was altered in the seventeenth and eighteenth century. Old pictures of the place show it to have been very picturesque with Gothic gables and tall clusters of chimneys.

At Castle Mill the upstream course of the Mole, with its various small tributaries, takes a generally south-eastern

*Castle Mill at Dorking, a large water-mill now converted as a private dwelling*

*Church Street, Betchworth, where cottages, church, and ancient barn combine to produce one of the county's most memorable scenes*

route and flows in lazy curves as it meanders along from across the Weald.

The river passes beneath the roadway just north of the village of Brockham where the large green is surrounded by a variety of old and not so old small houses and cottages that together form one of Surrey's finest village land-scapes.

I use the word 'landscape' here because the large green and the ever-changing colours of the great backcloth of the North Downs are very much part of the picture. But this is not all.

If one turns from the Downs and faces southwards, the green will be seen bounded by the most charming Vic-torian church. It was built in pale cream firestone with golden yellow limestone dressings by B. Ferrey in 1846. Small wonder that Brockham has been recognized as a conservation area of outstanding interest.

Nearby at Betchworth, Church Street is visually an important part of the village where the parish church terminates a cul-de-sac lined with seventeenth- and eighteenth-century cottages—some timber-framed—on one side, and a late seventeenth-century barn on the other. This barn has been neglected for a long time and is at present in a sorry state.

To the east of the church, through a Victorian 'postern' gate, is Priest's House which was built around 1630. Here is the kind of scene that Birket Foster—or Helen Alling-ham, that other watercolour painter who lived near Witley—may well have painted. A tile-hung gable, brick garden wall, a church tower and tall trees, it has all the ingredients they loved so much.

There is reason to suppose that Betchworth Church is on a Saxon site. A fragment of Saxon work survives in the form of a base or capital, built into an inner part of the south window of the Victorian tower.

It is supposed that a Norman tower was raised upon a Saxon chancel and a new chancel placed to the east. The remains of the chancel arch of this tower are now rebuilt into a narrow opening between the south aisle and the south chapel. This arch has been dated to *c.* 1080.

The church was further enlarged when north and south aisles were added—the nave arcades were built around 1200. The aisles were widened in the fourteenth century.

In the 1851 restoration, the Norman tower was re-moved and the present one built to the south. In 1870 the north transept was added and many windows renewed in egg-coloured stone; also the roofs were renewed, but the Horsham slab tiles were retained.

From Betchworth the road southwards to Leigh nego-tiates Snower Hill after passing the little timber-framed Fryleigh Cottages. Then it takes a route out across flat farmland where not so long ago the ways were impassable in bad weather.

Leigh is a tiny village with a green bounded by a

church, school and pub. Also, there is the Priest's House, a long range of timber-framed buildings that seem to be of fairly late construction. They are much restored and added to so that they look like a take-off by Lutyens or, perhaps, Shaw in an over-zealous vernacular style.

At Sidlow Bridge, west of Leigh, the Mole flows into Surrey from a part of the county transferred to Sussex and including Horley, Charlwood and Gatwick Airport.

There are, however, tributary streams that flow down to the Mole from the Holmwood and Capel area. These are crossed by a road that runs southwards from Leigh to Newdigate and beyond over the boundary to Rusper.

A mile along this road, past Little Shellwood, Mill Lane leads to Ewood where there was once a centre of the iron industry with, according to a survey of 1575, a furnace, forge and hammer, and also a mill for grinding corn.

The great mill-pond silted up long ago and is now cultivated. Mill Cottage, which stands near the stream, is an early seventeenth-century structure with panels of regular size and shape formed by the framing.

Nearby, is Ewood Farm of slightly earlier date. It is a house of three bays, and has much regular panelling that can be seen only at the back, as the front is tile-hung. There is a massive end stack of brick. Some farm buildings remain, including a seventeenth-century barn and a delightful small granary that is square in plan with a roof hipped on each side. Angle ties across the corners at eaves level are reminiscent of a similar structural device at Greens Farm, not far away, but they are here not an indication of great age as they are nearly always found in granaries of this type.

A little south of Ewood is Reffolds Copse, and back on the Newdigate Road, at the edge of this wood, is a nice continuous jetty cottage of the late sixteenth century with a fine end brick stack.

By retracing our tracks a little and then taking the road towards Charlwood, we cross the little Deanoak Brook and reach Highworth Farm in Stag Hill Road. This is a farm of moderate size with a farmyard and barns. It is a framed house of later sixteenth-century date, and is a good example of a house built with a centre smoke bay into which a brick chimney was subsequently built. This house is, in fact, one of the first examples of smoke-bay use to be identified many years ago before research into vernacular building had become a popular pastime.

Finally, at Newdigate, the church and the cluster of houses around the crossroads have been designated a conservation area. The church has been restored, but old work survives. The chancel with lancets is thirteenth century and the south arcade and south aisle are fourteenth century, but the best feature of the church is the restored fifteenth-century timber belfry at the west end. Both the north aisle and the east window are nineteenth century.

There are several notable houses in the village, in particular, Gaterounds Farm. The most important house, however, is a little outside the village. It is Greens Farm and is reached down a long drive off the road, from the village to the A24.

The house dates to around 1300 and is of the type shown in my figs. 1 and 2 in the Introduction. Because the house is so early it retains some archaic features—ties across two corners of the hall between tiebeam and wall-plates, long straight braces and an almost uniform use of timbers of square section. The roof is of crownpost construction and the centre of hall truss is especially fine with large braces beneath the cambered tiebeam, and all worked with a rich chamfer roll moulding.

Later, an upper floor was inserted into the hall, a crosswing was added after the removal of one end—possibly the parlour—and a brick chimney was added.

*Greens Farm at Newdigate is one of the most important early houses in the county and retains features in its construction that were outmoded even at the time of their use about 1300*

195

*Juniper Hall, once a haven for French émigrés, later the home of Mr Broadwood, the piano manufacturer*

CHAPTER FOURTEEN

# Stane Street

The Roman Stane Street was a military road built across the Weald about A.D. 60–70 to link London with Regnum—modern Chichester—then the capital of the Regnii and centre of the great wheat-producing lands in the Manhood.

The road was constructed on three alignments. Two radiated from London: one direct to Chichester and the other to Borough Hill, north-east of Pulborough. The third alignment was from Borough Hill to Chichester.

Leith Hill and the South Downs presented difficulties.

The Dorking Gap was the obvious route through the North Downs. Therefore, at Ewell the road left the London–Chichester alignment to cross the River Mole at Burford Bridge and emerge from the gap to pass east of Leith Hill and join the London-Borough Hill alignment at Ockley.

Stane Street had at least two branch roads: one was in Sussex, near Pulborough, and the other was mainly in Surrey, from Rowhook to Farley Heath. Both served settlements near the main route. The Surrey branch was on one alignment and ended at Jelley's Hollow, below Winterfold Hill.

The distance from London to Chichester along Stane Street was about sixty miles, and stations for the convenience of travellers are believed to have been at Merton, Dorking, Alfoldean and Hardman. Several known sites are near the road; Ewell is probably on the site of a small Roman town, and at Ashtead there was a villa and brickworks.

The present village of Ockley, once called Stane Street to distinguish it from the old Ockley settlement near the church on the Capel road to the north-east, is an obvious example of a settlement that has grown up in medieval times and was dependent upon the road.

Although modern roads coincide with Stane Street in only a few places, its alignments form a spine across the Weald upon which to build a description of the countryside and its settlements.

Stane Street was the first efficient road to penetrate the area where heavy clay and dense woodland made it almost impassable. When the Roman legions left, Stane Street deteriorated and the Weald once more became remote, its small settlements withdrawn and almost inaccessible within the dense woodlands.

Nonsuch, Ewell and Epsom have been mentioned in

previous chapters, therefore a convenient place to join the line of Stane Street now would be at Juniper Hall, Mickleham.

In 1787 the *Gentleman's Magazine* described Juniper Hall as being "on a spot where stood a little ale-house called Juniper Hole". The house was built by Sir Cecil Bisshopp and was "a bottom, at the foot of a hill, once a sheep-walk, but converted by him into a beautiful plantation, filled with beech, birch, ash, fir of various kinds, and other trees, disposed with great taste...." Then the *Gentleman's Magazine* continues, "From Pebble Lane the Roman Road ... is very visible on Mickleham Downs in several places for a considerable length".

Juniper Hall was later sold to a Mr Jenkinson and afterwards to Mr Broadwood, the piano manufacturer. In the late nineteenth century it was very much altered. An upper storey was added, and very ponderous 'Gothic' details including the 'railway station'—the local name for the cast iron *porte-cochère* which would be amusing elsewhere but is very off-putting here.

The interior of the house was remodelled, but a late eighteenth-century Adam-style dining-room was spared. This room is decorated with motifs forming panels surrounding large Wedgwood-inspired plaques with low relief figures on a pale blue ground.

The house is the property of the National Trust and is leased to the Field Studies Council.

During the French Revolution Juniper Hall was associated with French *émigrés*. Talleyrand, aristocrat, revolutionary and politician, who visited England twice—on one occasion to negotiate with Pitt—was a visitor to the hall for a short period.

General D'Arblay was also a resident and Fanny Burney, the royal attendant turned novelist, met him during a stay at Norbury Park. They fell in love and were married at Mickleham Church. After their marriage they lived at Great Bookham. Then they moved to a new house at West Humble purchased from the proceeds of Fanny's novel, *Camilla*, and named Camilla Lacey. The house was destroyed by fire.

Mickleham Church is north of Juniper Hall, and opposite the Running Horse Inn—a seventeenth-century house with part of its front covered in mathematical tiles—which was a popular place for stabling horses racing at Epsom. The church was restored in 1822–3 and again in 1872. The most attractive feature is the tower which has been much changed, but is Norman in origin. It has been lowered and massive buttresses have been added; it has a baleful clock face—like the eye of an owl—and a pretty, shingled spire. It is a fat, friendly tower!

Much of the interior is restoration work in a Norman style, but the windows on either side of the chancel are late Norman, of about 1180, with detached shafts and stiff leaf capitals—quite a contrast to the fake east window.

The Old House, south of the church, is in red brick with shaped gables and is dated 1636. The small gateway to the garden with pilasters and Ionic capitals—all in brick—is very typical of this style which owes much to Dutch influence.

Southwards from Juniper Hall, the modern road coincides with Stane Street for a short distance and passes near Flint Cottage. This nineteenth-century flint and brick house, so beautifully sited below Box Hill, was the home of George Meredith, the poet and novelist, until he died there in 1909.

Another poet, John Keats, was also at Box Hill for a short time. He stayed at the then much smaller inn at Burford Bridge to give him, as he says, "a spur to wind up my poem". The poem was *Endymion*.

At this same inn, in September, 1805, Lord Nelson rested for his last night in England on the journey that ended for him at Trafalgar. It is a remarkable coincidence that two of England's greatest, and most tragic, men should have both stayed at this place.

The line of Stane Street passes through Dorking to the south, and a short distance out of the town, along the Leith Hill road, is Mile House. This house has been altered, but it still has features identified with mid-seventeenth-century brickwork. The brick volutes at the upper windows are skilfully done. This is a house built by someone who wished to make a modest display by including features of

*St Michael's Church, Mickleham, was 'renovated' in 1823 by P.F. Robinson "in a style corresponding to its original character". Further work was done in 1872*

*Mile House, Dorking, a handsome house incorporating a modest use of mid-seventeenth-century decorative brickwork*

the fashionable brick style of his time, the style seen on a larger scale at the Old House, Mickleham.

Beyond Mile House, and near the great Iron Age earthworks of Anstiebury, the Roman road and the modern lane run together. This large fortified hill stands above the small village of Coldharbour where the houses are built of brownish-grey sandstone—the upper greensand of the area that passes in a narrow belt along the southern edge of the chalk Downs. The country is hilly and wooded, and from the precipitous margin of Anstiebury, which marks the southern edge of the greensand, the wide expanse of

the Weald extends far into Sussex.

Over the centuries the sides of Anstiebury Hill have been eroded by the weather. The planting of trees began in 1763—the few giant Wellingtonias growing there must date to this time. Much of the man-made fortification remains, however, and the series of ditches from the north-eastern side to the southern slopes can be seen clearly.

Many pathways lead through this area—as indeed is the case over much of the Weald—and from Coldharbour they fan out to Holmwood, Beare Green, and to Buckinghill Farm from where Stane Street and the modern road coincide for nearly two-and-a-half miles.

One of these pathways—to Holmwood—passes Trouts Farm, now a ruin. The large complex of barns and farmhouse have gone beyond all hope of repair, and it is sad to see a large medieval house so broken. Enough of the massive timbers remain to identify high quality work in the older part to which a later wing was added.

Ockley stands about midway along the stretch of Stane Street from Buckinghill Farm to near Halehouse Farm. The eastern side of the roadway is closely lined with houses, but to the west building has been kept far enough back to create a ribbon-like green.

At the northern end of the village, opposite the King's Arms, there is a tile-hung house, now made into two dwellings. It was built as a hall house and had a crosswing added to the north. There is a late extension—probably seventeenth century—to the south.

Much of the timber construction is covered with tile-hanging, but the Horsham tile roofs are exceptionally beautiful and clearly show the gradation of large to small tiles from the eaves to the ridge. The house has several bay, or oriel, windows each of which has a small roof, also of Horsham tiles.

Bordering the green are several framed houses. Lime Cottages, of sixteenth-century build, are flanked by matching additions with eighteenth-century-style Gothick windows. For what reason were these additions made, I wonder?

A group of cottages, near the Well Head which was erected about 1845, are framed houses of about 1600 that were so heavily overlaid with decorative work—in *cottage orné* style—in the nineteenth century that the old structure is almost completely concealed. These cottages are quite delightful flights of fancy, presumably estate work, which have made use of the old structure, especially the brick and stone chimney-stacks. The roofs are nineteenth century, built upon the raised walls of the original cottages.

The green is closed at the southern end by a weather-boarded house, The Tuns. It has a late eighteenth-century front of above average quality.

One-and-a-quarter miles south of Ockley, the modern main road veers south-easterly and leaves the line of Stane Street which continues its straight, south-westerly course for another 300 yards or so along a lane to Oakwoodhill. There the Roman road made a deviation to negotiate a steep incline. The first leg of this detour is also followed by the modern lane and continues, past the Georgian Hale-house Farm, down to a stream.

At this point the lane continues south-westerly but, after crossing the stream, the second leg of the Roman detour commenced with a sharp south-easterly turn. It ascended in a straight line along the terraced side of a precipitous hill, then turned again when it reached a point where it could come into line with the direction it had taken through Ockley.

Stane Street then continues on its straight course, and its line coincides with the driveway to Ruckmans for the last few hundred yards before it crosses a field into Sussex.

This area of Surrey, near the Sussex border, is still a place of large farmhouses. Some remain as the homes of farmers, but too many have ceased to be so.

A sixteenth-century house, Boswell Farm, near Oak-woodhill, is not lived in now—hounds are kept there—and it has not been 'restored' or made into what a city architect thinks a farmhouse should look like. It is kept (I trust) in a state of repair just sufficient to secure its continued existence. It has the appearance of a building in a Birket Foster watercolour, a 'genuine' appearance like that of scores of framed houses throughout the county a hundred years ago.

It would be very unrealistic to wish that the great wealth of Surrey's framed houses had been allowed to remain in a 'picturesque' condition. If they had, many would have fallen long ago, and if they are to be lived in, modern improvements have to be introduced.

Oakwood Church was a chapel of ease in this distant southern corner of the parish of Wotton and pathways radiate from it to many outlying communities. It was a single building, with nave and sanctuary under one roof, built in the early thirteenth century.

The church passed through various periods of neglect—by the authorities rather than the parishioners—but it has miraculously survived. In 1879 repairs were made and a north aisle was added, the thirteenth-century lancets from the old north wall being rebuilt into the new work.

The position of this small church, on a wooded hill above a brook with a bridge that carries a winding path up to the church, is remote even now. When standing in its quiet churchyard it is easy to imagine the complete isolation of the small communities dotted through this part of the Weald, even as recently as a hundred years ago.

Pollingfold, on the hill above the church, is a large framed house of about 1480. It has massive timbers and several unusual features including an interior jetty into the area that was once the open hall—of the kind described at Lee Crouch, Shamley Green.

Beneath this jetty, mortice holes for a plank bench once fixed to the wall between flanking doorways can be identified. Seats of this kind are known to have existed—usually for the master and his family at the high end of the hall—and are to be seen in fifteenth-century Flemish paintings. However, actual evidence of this kind is quite rare.

Woodham Cottage, on the road out of Oakwoodhill to Wallis Wood, is of light construction, being relatively late, but was framed in the traditional manner and was built with an end chimney-stack of brick.

The Farley Heath branch of Stane Street leaves the main route at Rowhook in Sussex and enters Surrey to the south-east of Ellens Green. It crosses Somersbury Lane, a little to the north of Bungtore Cottage, a late sixteenth-century framed cottage, built not as a hall house, but around a central brick chimney with front door and stair alongside.

The line of the Roman road runs westwards, almost parallel to the road linking Ewhurst Green and Ewhurst, and it passes very near to Slythurst. Once a farmhouse, it now has modern additions including a large wing of about 1880. The older part of the house is late sixteenth century and, like Bungtore Cottage, is a framed house built around a brick chimney.

West of Slythurst at the Swallow Tile works, hand-

*Pollingfold is a large fifteenth-century timber-framed house with a crownpost roof in which the rafters have been replaced this century, although the original rafters associated with each truss remain*

*A picturesque group of houses at Ewhurst combining work of several periods and a variety of traditional building materials*

made tiles are produced in an area noted for the quality of its brick earth. Several large brickworks are in the locality, and a Roman brickworks was found there in 1923 by members of Cranleigh School Archaeological Society.

Ewhurst Church was thoroughly worked over during the early nineteenth century when the tower was built in a Norman style by Robert Ebbels. The nave was probably less touched than the rest, and the south door is Norman. Although it is claimed to be the best piece of Norman decoration in Surrey, I cannot help feeling it has been altered and its original character very much lost by restoration.

The most picturesque corner of Ewhurst is at the northern end of the village, near the junction with the road to Forest Green, where stands a group of three houses—Old Farm, Debling Green and Windrums. The structures of these houses are closely interrelated and include work from the sixteenth century at the earliest.

Old Farm has the appearance of a high quality crosswing. It was jettied and has close-studding. The roof is of Horsham tiles and its construction has through purlins with angled struts, making use of re-used timber, probably from a crownpost roof. A stone outside stair to the first floor is an unusual feature in this context, and it might date to some period of decline when the house was used as a farm building.

Bramblehurst, along a driveway off Ockley Road, has

*The Swallow Tile Works, where much-sought-after handmade tiles are still produced*

been considerably restored in recent years, but has much original work including evidence of having been built as an open hall. A crosswing of about 1650 remains little altered and there is a very good large brick chimney-stack to which is attached an exceptionally fine bread oven, seen outside the house beneath its own roof.

Beyond Bramblehurst, along Ockley Road, is the small village of Forest Green with the hills of Hurtwood and Holmbury, with its Iron Age Fort, to the north.

Many interesting houses are in the area. Loseley, sixteenth century and once a farmhouse, is beautifully sited in fields north of Ockley Road and Cobbetts, in Lyefield

*Cobbetts, Forest Green, is a late sixteenth-century cottage with a larger addition of the late sixteenth century that had a raised eaves level to give added head-room in the attic*

Lane, is another sixteenth-century framed house, but with a good quality seventeenth-century crosswing.

The end of the Roman road is believed to be at Winterfold, and trackways would have extended the road up to Farley Heath, and the large site where there are extensive signs of early settlement and a Roman temple.

A little to the north-west, on Blackheath, is one of Norman Shaw's houses. Built in 1894–5, it has all the features typical of his work, but the front is more effective than the rear which lacks Shaw's usual distinctive touch.

It is, perhaps, appropriate that I should end with a Victorian house near a Roman road. Between the two epochs they represent is a span of time during which Surrey was blessed with very varied, if not always high quality, vernacular architecture.

Of the older houses that remain, most were farmhouses or cottages for those engaged in work associated with the land. Few so-called farmhouses are now the homes of farmers—the term is too often polite fiction.

There was much ecclesiastical building including the important abbeys of Chertsey and Waverley, although there was no cathedral until the present century.

The Victorians made a great impact upon the county. They restored the parish churches, nearly always with disastrous results, and with the coming of the railways the urbanization of the county began in earnest.

Norman Shaw's The Hallams typifies an aspect of this at

the upper level and anticipates the great impetus the growing demand for large houses gave to the career of the young Sir Edwin Lutyens. So highly do I regard this work in Surrey that in my list of half-a-dozen of the best houses in the county one would be by Lutyens and another by Norman Shaw.

*The Hallams, near Wonersh, a house by Norman Shaw, 1894–5, that shows his love of a large-scale porches and bay windows*

# Glossary

**Acanthus:** a conventional leaf form used in Classical decoration. Possibly first used by the Greeks about the time of the Peloponnesian War in the 'Corinthian' capital. Botanical connections appear to be tenuous.

**Aisle:** from the Latin *ala*—a wing. An outer, lateral division of a building appended to the main body.

**Alabaster:** gypsum (sulphate of lime). A stone principally taken from Derbyshire not unlike marble in appearance. It weathers badly and is unsuitable for external work. It is easy to work and allows a high degree of polish and detailed finish. Extensively used in church monuments in the later Middle Ages.

**Angled Strut:** *see* Strut.

**Angle Tie:** or dragon tie. 1. An archaic feature found in some very early buildings where it was used as a tie across the angle between the tiebeam and the wall plate. 2. Its later use, frequently in small granaries, was to tie the angles of the building, triangulation being further strength-ened by a short diagonal member binding it to the corner.

**Apse:** the termination of an architectural unit, such as a church, showing in plan as a half circle, a half ellipse or a half polygon.

**Arcade:** a row of free-standing posts (arcade posts) or piers (arcade piers), supporting an upper structure, usually of arches, or in a timber-framed building, an arcade plate (q.v.). A blind arcade is the same but stands against a wall.

**Arcade Plate:** a horizontal timber passing across the heads of the posts in an arcade.

**Architrave:** in Classical architecture it is a member of the upper structure immediately above the column and below the frieze (q.v.).

**Baluster:** a vertical member of an identical series support-ing a coping or handrail and thus forming a balustrade.

**Bargate Stone:** a sandstone found in the Godalming area, of a warm brown colour caused by the presence of iron. It can be built in courses, but is more often used as rubble stone.

**Barge-Board:** a board, one of a pair, usually, but not necessarily, carved. With its face in a vertical plane it is attached along the whole length of the gable end of a roof and follows the terminal edge of the roof covering.

**Bay:** a division in a framed building limited by the prin-cipal posts (q.v.) and the principal roof trusses (q.v.). It is also an external lateral division defined by the fenestration.

**Belvedere**: a small building in a park or garden erected expressly for the purpose of enjoying a fine prospect.

**Bond**: the arrangement in which bricks are laid. The three most common are: Header bond in which every course is laid with bricks placed end on; English bond in which the courses of header bricks alternate with courses of stretchers, i.e. bricks laid lengthways; Flemish bond in which every course is laid with alternate headers and stretchers arranged so that headers occur centrally between stretchers in alternate courses.

**Bower**: room in a house set apart for the family, originally for the primary use of the women; or a sleeping place above the service end in a small open hall house.

**Brace**: in a framed structure, can be straight, curved or ogee. It is set to strengthen the angle between two other members. Can be used in compression, or in later work, tension.

**Bressumer**: beam supporting a structure above an opening, also the beam upon which the projecting joists of a jetty rest.

**Build**: a currently accepted noun derived from the verb to build, used to refer to a construction, or part of a construction, erected at any one time. A complete building may comprise several builds.

**Butt Side Purlin**: a purlin placed between principal rafters, in fact not butted, but jointed by mortice and tenon (q.v.). *See* Introduction.

**Buttery**: from old Flemish *boterie*, a drink store.

**Caen Stone**: a limestone from the Caen region of Normandy in France.

**Camber**: in a tiebeam, slight curve or arch so that the centre is higher than the ends.

**Capital**: of a column, can be carved or be comprised of mouldings.

**Canopy of grace—Celure**: panelled, or specially decorated area of a church roof above a rood-screen (q.v.).

**Carstone**: hard stone from the Lower Greensand, an iron oxide content gives it a dark brown colour. Suitable for use as rubble also for galleting (q.v.).

**Casement**: window hinged on one vertical edge, opens either inwards or outwards.

**Centre Purlin**: *see* Introduction.

**Chamfer**: a bevel formed by the removal of the angle of a squared timber or stone.

**Chancel**: a part of a church east of the nave and containing the altar.

**Chancel Arch**: an arch standing between the nave and the chancel.

**Choir**: the part of the church where the services are sung.

**Cladding**: material used externally as a covering to a wall.

**Close Studding**: vertical intermediate timbers in a wall of a framed structure placed little more than their own width apart, usually for decoration.

**Clunch:** hard form of chalk capable of being carved and used as a building stone, weathers badly when used externally.

**Coade Stone:** very durable artificial stone of unknown composition used for casting architectural ornament, popular from about 1770 until around 1836.

**Collar Beam:** *see* Introduction.

**Collar Purlin:** synonymous with centre purlin, *see* Introduction.

**Collegiate Church:** foundation by a wealthy individual, to be distinguished from a cathedral or monastery, governed by canons for the purpose of offering prayers for the repose of the soul of the founder.

**Colonnade:** row of columns supporting a superstructure, *see* arcade.

**Continuous Jetty:** a jetty (q.v.) running along the full length of the side of a framed house.

**Corbel:** a projection provided to support a weight.

**Corinthian:** a Classical order with fluted column and carved capital employing acanthus leaf (q.v.) motif.

**Cornice:** upper projecting section of an entableture (q.v.) in Classical architecture; also decorated termination to the top of a wall.

**Cross Passage:** *see* Introduction.

**Crosswing:** *see* Introduction.

**Crownpost:** *see* Introduction.

**Cupola:** a Classical feature, a domed turret crowning a roof.

**Diaper:** in brickwork the formation of an all-over pattern, often diamond, by using bricks of a different colour to those of the main wall surface.

**Ditterling Gate:** so called by John Aubrey (*see* bibliography), a style based upon the published designs of a German, Wendel Dietterlin.

**Dog-Tooth:** decoration consisting of a row of small pyramidal forms cut to represent four leaves.

**Doric:** a Classical order, its most famous use is to be found in the Athenian Parthenon.

**Dormer:** a window set vertically in a roof, with its own roof.

**Double Pile:** house plan of seventeenth- and eighteenth-century origin of more than one room deep and placed beneath separate parallel roofs. Its purpose was to avoid the prominence of a single roof of greater height for aesthetic and structural reasons.

**Dressings:** work placed around openings, e.g. doors and windows, often of a material superior to that of the main structure, to provide a finish.

**Dripstone:** moulding placed above a door or window to throw off the rain. Known also as a hood mould, or when rectangular in outline as a label.

**Dutch Gable:** *see* gable.

**Early English:** the first period of English Gothic architecture following the Transitional period, from about 1189 until

1272 during the reigns of Richard I, John, and Henry III.

**Easter Sepulchre:** symbolic tomb within a recess, or beneath a canopy, to represent the Tomb of Christ, and prominent at the Easter services.

**Eaves Cornice:** projecting upper termination to a wall, moulded or carved, set at the over-hang of a pitched roof.

**Entableture:** the whole of the horizontal members above a column in Classical architecture, comprises architrave, frieze and cornice.

**Firestone:** calcareous sandstone synonymous with Reigate or Merstham stone (q.v.) so-called because of its fire- and heat-resisting properties.

**First Floor Hall:** principal room in a medieval hall house raised to the first floor.

**Floored:** containing an upper floor, or to have received an inserted floor as a later addition.

**Framed:** constructed of timber, jointed together to form an open framework that is infilled with other material.

**Frieze:** horizontal division beneath the cornice (q.v.) in Classical architecture, often moulded or carved.

**Gable:** triangular area of a wall closing the end of a ridged roof. A Dutch gable has a curved profile rising in front of the roof and is crowned by a pediment (q.v.). A shaped gable is the same but lacks the pediment.

**Gablet:** set above the hipped end of a roof, a small triangular area formed by an upper (gablet) collar framed between the terminal rafters at the meeting with the hip rafters.

**Galleried:** containing an upper open passage across the front giving access to a series of rooms.

**Galleting, Garneting:** small chips of stone or flint set into wide mortar joints while still wet to save the mortar from the action of weather. Also has a decorative purpose as internal use has been found.

**Garderobe:** a lavatory or privy.

**Gothic Revival:** interest in medieval art that commenced in the eighteenth century and flourished in the nineteenth. In architecture it produced work that simulated the appearance of the original, but not the spirit.

**Gothick:** term applied to fanciful interpretations of Gothic styles.

**Half-Timbering:** synonymous with timber-framed and framed (q.v.).

**Hall:** principal room in a medieval house (*see* Introduction), later became of less importance and now survives as the area into which a main entrance opens.

**Hammer-Beam Roof:** form of roof capable of covering a width comparable to that of an aisled building. Arcade posts (q.v.) are dispensed with by the use of short bracketed beams (hammer-beams) at wall-plate (q.v.) level that support posts (hammer-posts) set beneath the purlins.

**Header:** *see* Bond.

**Hip:** sloping section of roof closing the end of a building and extending from an end tiebeam, or wall plate, (full hip), or from a collar beam (half hip) to the apex or gablet (q.v.).

**Horsham Slab:** also referred to as slates or tiles. Sandstone quarried in the Wealden clay in the Horsham area.

**Ionic:** Classical order distinguished by a voluted capital.

**Ironstone:** synonymous with carstone.

**Jetty:** projection formed by the extension of floor joists so that an upper floor overhangs a lower.

**Jowl:** *see* Introduction.

**Keep:** strongly fortified tower in a castle designed to be both a residence and a place of last resort in case of attack.

**King-Post:** vertical post extending from a tiebeam to the apex of a roof. King-strut, the same but extending only to beneath a beam along the ridge. Both forms unusual in pre-nineteenth-century Surrey.

**Lancet:** narrow window opening with a pointed head of the Transitional and Early English styles (q.v.).

**Lap:** joint formed by one member overlapping a part of another.

**Lesene:** associated with Saxon architecture, flat or shallow projection attached to a stone wall, said to be a decoration originating from timber construction, but may also be intended to add strength to the wall.

**Lunette:** as applied to a window, half-moon shaped.

**Manor:** unit of land and its associated social group managed under the authority of a lord of the manor.

**Mathematical Tiles:** so made that when they are hung on battens, or embedded in plaster, they can be pointed up to be indistinguishable from brickwork.

**Manhood:** Hundred of Manhood, comprising the Selsey Peninsular.

**Merstham Stone:** synonymous with Reigate stone and firestone (q.v.), a sandstone favoured by masons because of its easy working qualities, similar to Caen stone (q.v.) but it weathers very badly.

**Modillion:** small projecting bracket, usually close set in a continuous row to form an optical relief in the deep shadow beneath a Classical cornice.

**Mortice and Tenon:** most common joint in English carpentry since the Romanesque period, *c.*twelfth century, in which the tongue (tenon) on one section is inserted into the socket (mortice) in the other.

**Mullion:** vertical dividing bar in a window opening.

**Nave:** in a church, the main body of the building for the use of the laity.

**Newel:** central post around which a stair is constructed; or the principal posts in a staircase between which the balusters and baluster rails are placed.

**Ogee:** a double curve, concave passing to convex.
**Open Hall:** *see* Introduction.
**Oriel:** bay window extending upwards from the ground, or supported at a higher level by brackets.
**Orné:** fanciful style based upon an imaginary, idealized, conception of rustic architecture.
**Outshot, Outshut:** a lean-to or extension at the rear of a house.

**Palladian:** style of architecture based upon the work and writings of Andrea Palladio 1518–80.
**Pantry:** from Old French *paneterie*, food store.
**Parallel Bracing:** *see* Introduction.
**Parapet:** low wall to afford protection from a drop, on a bridge or house top.
**Parclose Screen:** divides a side chapel from the rest of the church.
**Pediment:** triangular shape above the entableture of a Classical portico or opening.
**Petworth Marble:** synonymous with Sussex marble. Found in thin veins no more than six inches thick, a shelly (genus Palundina) limestone of the Wealden clay.

Much used for paving, also for monuments.
**Pilaster:** shallow pier of rectangular section attached to a wall.
**Piscina:** basin placed near the altar for washing the chalice, set in the wall and often the subject of decorative treatment, provided with a drain that soaks away within the wall.
**Principal Posts:** main upright timbers that extend to the full height of a timber frame.
**Portico:** Classical feature at an entrance composed of columns, either attached or detached, and supporting an entableture (q.v.) often with a pediment (q.v.).
**Puddingstone:** conglomerate of pebbles and grit held together with ferrous material, a poor building stone used as a last resort.
**Purlin:** centre purlin, side purlin, *see* Introduction.
**Puthole:** or putlock hole, in a wall to take the putlock or short horizontal bar of a scaffold, the holes may be filled, closed with a stone, or left open.
**Putto (Putti):** small naked child figure(s) used in sculptural compositions and in paintings, synonymous with *amorini*.

**Quatrefoil:** applied to an aperture, or arch, containing cusps that break it into four leaf shapes. Trefoil and cinquefoil have three and five divisions respectively.
**Quoin:** dressed corner stone of a wall.

**Rafter:** *see* Introduction.

**Reigate Stone:** synonymous with Merstham Stone (q.v.).

**Reredos:** structure of both decorative and religious content behind and above—but not attached to—an altar.

**Roll Moulding:** a rounded moulding approaching a complete circular section to a greater or lesser degree.

**Rood:** crucifix or cross. Rood-loft, a gallery above a rood-screen which is placed between the nave and the chancel.

**Rubbers:** soft bricks of good quality which can be sawn and rubbed to an exact shape (gauged work) for use at openings or where fine joints are required. May be in contrasting colour to the rest of the work e.g. red rubbers.

**Sandstone:** stone composed of consolidated sand. Varies considerably in colour and durability.

**Sans-Purlin:** a roof in which there are no purlins.

**Sarsen Stone:** synonymous with heathstone and greyweather. In Surrey, sandstone boulders found on, or just beneath, the heaths, remnants conveyed from once more complete layers of sandstone. From the word saracen—a stranger.

**Scalloped:** decoration derived from the scallop shell—a series of segments of circles.

**Scissor Brace:** *see* Introduction.

**Screens Passage:** synonymous with crosspassage, *see* Introduction.

**Scratch Dial:** mass dial, a small sun-dial with a central hole to take a gnomon, of pre-Reformation date and used by a priest to determine the canonical hours.

**Sedilia:** seats for the celebrant and two assistants on the south side of the chancel of a church.

**Shaped Gable:** *see* gable.

**Shingle:** cleft oak tile, cut with a thick upper edge and a thin lower one—used on roofs and walls.

**Shell Keep:** walled enclosure on a mound or motte for the purpose of defence.

**Shaft:** in medieval architecture a slender column; in Classical architecture the member of a column between the capital and the base.

**Smoke Bay:** *see* Introduction.

**Spandrel:** triangular space between the outer curve of an arch and the rectangle formed by the mouldings enclosing it.

**Spere:** short wooden screen at the side of a doorway to reduce the draught.

**Squint:** hole cut in a wall to give a view of the main altar.

**Stiff-Leaf:** early form of carved leaf developed through the Transitional period (q.v.) and perfected in the Early English (q.v.).

**Strut:** intermediary roof timber supporting a beam; it may be vertical (queen strut), or set at an angle (angle strut) to support a purlin when the collar is omitted.

**Sussex Marble:** *see* Petworth marble.

**Studs—Studding:** intermediate vertical timbers set in a wall frame.

**Tenon:** *see* mortice and tenon.

**Tiebeam:** *see* Introduction.

**Tile-Hanging:** wall covering of overlapping tiles hung on battens, may be used over a brick or framed wall as a protection against weather, or in the latter case as cladding.

**Timber-Framing:** *see* framed.

**Transept:** north and south transverse arms in a church with a cruciform plan.

**Trefoil:** *see* quatrefoil.

**Tuscan Order:** a modified form of the Doric order (q.v.).

**Turnpike:** began with an Act in 1663 allowing Justices of the Peace to erect gates (turnpikes) and charge tolls for the purpose of improving and maintaining roads.

**Transitional:** period of change, notably that from Norman Romanesque to English Gothic.

**Truss:** principal framework of a roof, designed to support other members, and set at bay (q.v.) intervals.

**Volute:** decorative motif in the form of a spiral scroll.

**Wall-Plate:** horizontal timber at the top of a wall (stone, brick or framed) from which the rafters are pitched.

**Wealden House:** type of hall house with continuous eaves in which the end bays only are jettied forward thus creating the illusion of a recessed centre. Most common in the Weald, but of wide distribution elsewhere.

**Weather-Boarding:** horizontal overlapping feather-edged boards covering a framed wall.

**Wind-Braces:** strengthening timbers placed between a side purlin and a principal rafter. May be curved or straight or decoratively treated. *See* Introduction.

# Bibliography

Addy, Sidney Oldall, *Evolution of the English House*, 2nd edn, 1933. Republished E. P. Publishing Ltd., 1975

Aubrey, John, *Natural History and Antiquities of the County of Surrey*, 1718–19, 5 vols. Republished Kohler and Coombes, 1975

Brayley, E.W., *History of Surrey*, 4 vols, 1878

Brunskill, R.W., *Illustrated Handbook of Vernacular Architecture*, Faber, 1970

Chamberlin, E.R., *Guildford, a Biography*, Macmillan, 1970

Clifton-Taylor, Alec, *The Pattern of English Building*, Faber, 1972

Clifton-Taylor, Alec, and Brunskill, R.W., *English Brickwork*, Ward Lock, 1977

Cobbett, William, *Rural Rides*, 1830. Penguin Books Edition, 1967

Davie, W.G., and Green, Curtis W., *Old Cottages and Farmhouses in Surrey*, Batsford, 1908

Dugmore, R., *Puttenham under the Hog's Back*, Phillimore, 1972

The Gentleman's Magazine Library, Surrey—Sussex 1900.

Gravett, K., *Timber and Brick Building in Kent*, Introductory essay, Phillimore, 1971

Hewitt, C.A., *The Development of Carpentry, An Essex Study*, David and Charles, 1969

Jekyll, G., *Old West Surrey*, 1904. Republished Kohler and Coombes, 1978

Kohler, M.K., (editor) *Memories of Old Dorking*, Kohler and Coombes, 1977

Lloyd, Nathaniel, *A History of English Brickwork*, republished Blom, 1972

Lloyd, Nathaniel, *A History of the English House*, republished Architectural Press, 1975

Malden, H.E., (editor) *The Victoria History of the County of Surrey*

Manning, Revd Owen, and Bray, W., *The History and Antiquities of the County of Surrey*, published 1804, 1809, 1814

Mason, R.T., *Framed Buildings of the Weald*, Coach Publishing House Ltd., 1969

Mason, R.T., *Framed Buildings of England*, Coach Publishing House Ltd.

Nevill, R., *Old Cottage and Domestic Architecture in South-West Surrey*, 1889

O'Connor, M., *The History of Effingham*, Effingham Women's Institute, 1973

Parker, E., *Highways and Byways in Surrey*, Macmillan, 2nd edn, 1950

Percy, K., and Gray, P., (editors of series) *Lingfield, Godstone, Limpsfield, Oxted, Bletchingley* and *Chaldon*, published by Tandridge District Council

Pevsner, N., and Nairn, I., *The Buildings of England, Surrey*, 2nd edn, Penguin, 1971

Salzman, L.F., *Building in England down to 1540*, Oxford, 1967

Stevens, L.R., *A Village of England, Byfleet*, Livrevin Promotion and Services Ltd., 1972

Surrey County Council, *List of Antiquities and Conservation Areas in Surrey* 6th edn, 1976

Temple, N., *Farnham Buildings and People*, Phillimore, 1973

Wood, M., *The English Medieval House*, Phoenix, 1965

Wight. J., *Brick Building in England*, John Baker, 1972

# *Index*

Dates of births and deaths, or periods when known to have been working, are given for architects, authors and artists. In the case of monarchs the dates refer to the periods of their reigns. Heavy type indicates the page number of an illustration.

**A3,** 153
A24, 81
A25; 17, 73, 81, 90, 94, 95, 96, 114
A30, 157, 158
Abbot, George, Archbishop of Canterbury, (1562–1633), 33, 35
Abinger, 77–9; Crossways Farm, 21, **78**
Abinger Hammer, 74–7
Adam, Robert, architect, (1728–92), 45, 48, 55; Adamesque (style of), 61, 198
Aisled hall, *see* HALL
Albury, 69–70; Cookes Place **70;** downs, 69; old church, 71
Aldebury, 67, 128
Alexander I of Russia, 150
Alfold, 131, 134; Alfold House, 134, **134;** Bookers Lee, 134; church, **135,** 136; Crossways, 134; Sidney Wood, 131, 137
Alfoldean, 197
Allingham, Helen, artist, (1848–1926), 193
Anchoress, 73
Angle tie, 194, 195, 209
Anjou, Margaret of, 111
Anne of Denmark, 124

Apse, 30, 209
Arcade post, 17, 24, 25, 96, 209
Arnold, Matthew, (1822–88), 146, 175
Artington: Old Friars, 149
Ash, 169; Hartshorn Cottage and Church, **168**
Ashford, 172
Ashtead Church, 45; park, 45
Attlee, W., 83
Aubertin, Peter, and son Peter, 104
Aubrey, John, antiquary, (1626–97), 36, 83, 120, 124, 189
Augusta Ada, Lady Lovelace, 52
Austen, Godwin, 61
Austen, Robert, 27
Austin Canons, 67, 87, 128
Avenel, clockmaker, 33
Aylward, clockmaker, 18

**Bacon, J., sculptor, (1740–99),** 61
Bagshot, 157; park, 159
Baker, Thomas, 35
Banstead, 99–104; Banstead Wood, **100;** downs, 99; Woodmans Cottage, **98**
Barracks, military, 157
Barrett, George, 190
Barrie, Sir James M., (1860–1937), 110
Barry, Sir Charles, architect, (1795–1860), 52
Bay, 13, 209
Beare Green, 200
Beaufort, Margaret, 128
Beckingham, John, 36
Bells, 105; belfrey, 154, 163, 194; bell-turret, 115, 137
Belvedere, 146, 210
Betchworth, 192–3; castle, 190
Bicycle, 149
Bisham Abbey, 159
Bisshopp, Sir Cecil, 198
Blackheath, 206; The Hallams, **207**
Black Prince, 124
Bletchingley, 90–4, **91,** 115; Brewer

Street, 93; Pendell Court, 93; Pendell House, 93
Blomfield, Sir Arthur, architect, (1829–99), 35, 150
Blomfield, Sir Reginald, R.A., (1856–1942), 123
Bond, 210. *See also* BRICK
Bonomi, Joseph, architect, (1739–1806), 45
Bonsor, Joseph, 50
Borough Hill, 197
Boscawen, Admiral, 55
Bosworth Farm, 201
Botleys Park, 160, **161**
Bower, 13, 210
Box Hill, 80–81, 189, 190, 199
Brace, 210; arch, 154; crossed, 115; curved, 74; decorative, 131, 138, 149, 152; ogee, 65, 134; parallel, 96, 137; passing, 24; transverse, 15; wind, **12,** 216
Bramley: East Manor House, 74, 131; Nursecombe Farm, 65, 131; Snowdenham, 131
Bray, William, antiquary, (1736–1832), 77
Bressumer, 141, 210
Brett, John, artist, (1830–1902), 190
Brick, 17, 210; black headers, 147; blue headers, 115; 'decorative' style, 13, 21, 25, 50, 61, 79, 80, 152, 188, 199, **200;** diaper, 18, 211; polychrome, 107, 165, 175; porch, 166; red rubbers, 165; refronting, 55, 95, 116, 137, 149, 154, **155,** 165; stair, 144; yellowstock, 107, 185; fifteenth century, 17, 144; sixteenth century, 173, 179; seventeenth century, 75, 83, 185, 187, 199; eighteenth century, 50, 64, 165, 173, 182
Bridgeman, Charles, 146
Brighton railway, 89
Broadstreet Common, 166. *See also* WORPLESDON

Broadwood, J., piano manufacturer, 198
Brockham, 193
Brook, 154
Brook Farm, nr Tandridge, 115
Brooklands, 123; Brooklands motor race track, 124
Brookwood: cemetery, 163
Brown, L. 'Capability', architect and landscape gardener, (1715–83), 146
Brown and Holland, 146
Buckingham Farm, 200
Buckland, 84; green, **85**
Burford Bridge, 190, 197, 199
Burne-Jones, E., artist, (1833–93), 89
Burney, Fanny, novelist, (1752–1840), 198
Burningfold Farm, 133. *See also* DUNSFOLD
Burnt Common, 55
Burpham, 149; Burpham Court Farm, 127
Burstow, 120–21; church, **121**
Butler, John, 134
Butterfield, William, architect, (1814–1900), 107
Buttery, 13, 50, 62, 210
Buxted, Sussex, 134
Byfleet, 124; Byfleet Court Rolls, 50
Byron, Hon. John, 165
Byron, Lord, 52
Bysshe, Edward, 122

**Caen stone,** 104
Calva, Ruald de, 128
Canals: Basingstoke, 124, 162, 169; Godalming Navigation, 138; Wey-Arun, 123, 131, 137; Wey Navigation, 124, 127, 131
Canopy of grace (celure), 127, 210
Carpenter, Christine, 73
Carroll, Lewis, author, (1832–98), Cheshire Cat, 133
Carron Ironworks, 134

Carter, Francis, 29, 38
Carwarden, Thomas, 120
Caterham, 107–8; Arthur's Seat, 110; folly, 110; Quarry Hanger Hill, 110
Caterham-on-the-Hill, 107
Catershall Mill, 141
Chaldon, 105–7; church, **106**
Chalk, 116; clunch fireplaces, 38, 150; clunch walling, 128, 160
Chambers, Sir William, architect, (1726–98), 141
Charles I, (1625–49), 123
Charles II, (1660–85), 129
Charlotte, Princess, 146
Charlwood, 194
Chaucer, Geoffrey, (c. 1340–1400), 147
Chelsham, 113
Chequer work, flint and brick, 44
Chertsey, 173–6; abbey, 159–60; bridge, 160, **174**; Curfew House, **175**; Hamm Moor, 123; museum and Little Cedars, **177**
Chichester, 197
Chiddingfold, 131, 137, 153; Combe Court Farm, 137; Crown Inn, **138**; Hawlands, 138; Imbhams, 138; Killinghurst, 138
Child, John, 34; son of, 22
Chilworth, 66; manor, 67, **69**
Chimney: brick, 15, 150, 205; central, 15, 202; crow-stepped, 139; end, 15, 115, 194, 202; later insertion, 15, 64, 95, 194, 195; nineteenth-century ornamental, 69; side, 15, 66
Chipstead, 99, 103; church, **102**
Chobham, 160; common, 157
Christmas, Gerard, John and Matthias, sculptors, (working c. 1620s), 35
Cipriani, G. B., painter, (1727–85), 190
Cistercians, 21
Civil War, 18
Clandon Park, 55, **57**, **58**, **59**
Clare, Earl of, 146

Clare family, 93
Claremont. See ESHER
Claremont School Trust Ltd., 146
Clayton, Robert, 90
Cleveland, Barbara Duchess of, 129
Cleves, Anne of, 93
Clinton, Henry, Earl of Lincoln, 123
Clive of India, 146
Close studding, 169, 205
Cloth manufacture, 30, 33, 40, 73, 174
Clunch. See CHALK
Coaching inns, 146, 147, 150. See also GUILDFORD
Coade stone, 87
Coalbrookdale, 134
Cobbett, William, author, (1762–1835), 18; *Rural Rides*, 66
Cobham, 146, 186, 187; Ham Manor, **186**; Pains Hill Park, 146, 186
Cobham family, 95, 119, 120
Codington, Richard, 43
Coldharbour, 200
Collar, **12**, 15
Colman, Jeremiah, jun., 111
Colnbrook, 172
Compton, 26; White Hart Cottage, **27**
Cooper, Sir Edwin, 111
Cosford Mill, 154
Cottage orné. See ORNÉ
Couse, Kenton, architect, (1721–90), 160
Cranleigh, 64, 131, 132, 133; church **133**
Crawley, George, 116
Crécy, 119
Crossland, W. H., architect, (fl. 1880s), 157
Cross passage, 17, 50, 62, 134, 150, 179
Crosswing, **12**, 15, 55, 65, 70, 153, 205; added, 73, 74, 120, 129, 130, 131, 134, 137, 138, 139, 154, 160, 162, 179, 195, 200, 206; brick, 162, 165, 166; set at right angles, 94, 95. See also JETTY
Crowhurst, 115, 116

Crownpost, **12**, 15, 24, 50, 55, 64, 65, 70, 84, 90, 107, 108, 121, 134, 137, 139, 149, 165, 188, 195, 205; obsolete, 120
Croydon, 113
Cubitt, Thomas, architect, (1788–1855), 50, 80
Cuddington, 43
Cumberland, Duke of, 158
Currie, W., 52

**D'Abernon, Richard,** 69
D'Arblay, General, 198
Dartford, James, architect, 150
Day, Frances, 146
Deanoak Brook, 194
Dedeswell Manor, 55
Defoe, D., author, (1660–1731), 189
Delius, Frederick, (1862–1934), 96
Department of the Environment, 22
Devil's Punch Bowl, 154
Dickens, Charles, author, (1812–70), 83, 152, 173
Dissolution Act, 22, 113, 115, 120, 127, 128, 173
Ditterling Gate, 124, **125**, 211
Dog-tooth moulding, 30
Doric columns, 45
Dorking, 81, 82, 83, 84, 189, 190, 199; gap, 197; Lime Company, 84; Mile House, **200**; parish church, **82**
Double pile, 99, 211
Downs, north, 67, 90, 105, 113, 189
Dragon beam, 27
Drummond, Henry, banker, 69
Dunsfold, 131, 133, 137, 154; Oak Tree Cottage, **136**
Dyball, Sextus, 111

**Earthwork,** 96
Eashing, 141; bridge, **140**
East Clandon, 55; Tunmore Cottage, **55**
Easter sepulchre, 181
East Horsley, 51, 52; Manor House, **52**;

Towers, **51**
East India Company, 67
East Molesey, 181, 185; Bell Inn, **184**
Eaves cornice, 93, 130, 212
Eaves cruck, 141, 149
Ebbels, Robert, architect, (d. 1860), 205
Effingham, 50
Egham, 157
Eldeberie, 69
Eliot, George, authoress, (1819–80), 153
Elizabeth I, (1558–1603), 43, 123, 124
Elmbridge Borough Council, 146
Elstead, 141
Ember, River, 185
*Emigrés*, 198
Englefield Green, 157, 158
Epsom, 44, 45; downs, 99, 100, 197, 198; Princes Stand, **44**
Esher, 143, 144; Claremont, **145**, 146; St George's Chapel, 143, **143**; Waynflete Tower, 144, **144**, 185
Evelyn family, 79, 93; Evelyn Chapel, Wotton, 80
Evelyn, John, diarist, 36, 79, 83, 87
Evelyn, John and George, 69
Evelyn, W., 77

**Fairmile,** 146
Falkner, Harold, architect, (1875–1963), 18, 21; Burles Lodge, 21; Dippenhall estate, 21; Moor Park, 22
Farleigh, 113; church, 114
Farley Heath, 64, 197, 202, 206
Farncombe: Wyatt Almshouses, 150
Farnham, 17, 18, 21, 110, 138, 141, 188; castle, **16**; Willmer House, **19**
Felbridge, 93
Ferguson Gang, 61
Fernhurst, Sussex, 134
Ferrey, B., architect, (1810–80), 18, 61, 193
Fetcham, 48; church, **48**
Field Studies Council, Juniper Hall, 198

Firebacks, 116, 134
Fitzwilliam, Sir William, Earl of Southampton, 22
Flamstead, John, F.R.S., Astronomer Royal, (1646–1719), 121
Flint, 29, 55, 104, 107, 176
Flint Cottage, 199
Folly, 110
Font, 137, 103, 154, 176
Forest Green, 205; Cobbetts, **206**
Forster, Anne, 115–16
Foster, Myles Birket, painter, (1825–99), 153, 193, 201
Frampton, Sir George, R.A., sculptor, (1860–1928), 186
Frederick William, King of Prussia, 150
Frensham, 138, 141; ponds, 142
Friday Street, 77
Frimley Green, 169
Frosbury Farmhouse, 166
Fry, Roger, art critic, (1866–1934), 40
Fuller's earth, 90
Fulling mills, 30

**Gable**, 212; Dutch, 166, 185, 188; shaped, 199
Gablet, 25, 64, 212
Galleting, (garneting), 79, 165, 212
Gambrel roof, 119
Garderobe, 30, 212
Gaynesford, Thomas, 115
*Gentleman's Magazine*, 198
George II, (1726–60), 158
George IV, (1820–30), 159
Ghent, Benedictine monastery, 111
Gibbet Hill, 154–6
Gibbons, Grinling, woodcarver, (1648–1720), 18
Gibson, John, architect, (fl. 1870s), 89
Glass industry, 111
Glyd, Richard, 93
Godalming, 131, 139, 150, 152; Cider House, 141, 149; Godalming Naviga-tion, 138; Town Hall (Pepper Pot), **152**
Godstone, 93; White Hart, **92**
Gomshall, 74; King John House, **75**; Malthouse Cottages, **76**
Goodchild, Thomas, architect, 30
Gothic, Commissioners', 40, 45, 201
Gothick, 83, 84, 144, 212
Granary, 142, 194, 209
Grange, Hampshire, 69
Grantley family, 62
Grasshopper Inn, 96
Great Bookham, 48, 198
Great Fire, 43
Great Tangley Manor, 62, 74
Greek style, 83–4
Greens Farm, Newdigate, 194, **195**
Greensand, 90
Greville, Mrs, 50
Guildford:
    Churches: cathedral, **41, 42**; Holy Trinity, 29, 35; St Mary, 30, **31**; St Nicolas, 42; Stoke Church, 40
    Inns: Angel Hotel and undercroft, 36; Red Lion, 36; Stoke Hotel, 40; White Hart, 36; White Lion, 36
    Locations: Bellfields, 127; Bury Fields, 40; Dominican Friary, 36; Epsom Road, 40; Farnham Road, 26; Guildown, 26, 42; Millbrook, 28–9; North Street, 34; North Town Ditch, 33; Portsmouth Road, 40, 42; Rosemary Alley, 28; Stag Hill, 42; Stoke Park, 127; Stoke Road, 40; Wharfs, tread-wheel, 124; Undercroft, No. 72, High Street, 36
    Other buildings: Caleb Lovejoy Almshouses, **39**, 42; Castle House, 38; Cloth Hall, 34; Durbins, 40; Parson's Alms-houses, 40; Rectory Place, 42; Somerset House, 38; Villas,
Portsmouth Road, 40
    Public Buildings: Castle Arch, Museum and Muniment Room, **28**, 38; Castle Keep, **29**, 29; George Abbot's Hospital, 33, **34**; George Abbot Schools, 34; Guildford House, 34, **35**
    Shops: Corona Restaurant (Pizzaland) **38**, 38; Sainsburys, 36; Timothy Whites, 36; Wool-worths, 36
Guild Merchant, 33
Gunpowder, 66, 67, 93
Guns, 116; gunshot, 116, 138
Gwilt, George, county surveyor, (1767–1825), 150, 189

**Hakewell, E.C., architect, (1812–72)**, 69
Halehouse Farm, Ockley, 200–201
Half Moon, 154
Hall, **12**, 13, 62, 65, 73, 74, 84, 93, 94, 95, 96, 100–103, 116, 129, 130, 131, 134, 137, 139, 141, 149, 154; aisled 17, 137; first floor, 162, 166, 200
Hamilton, Hon. Charles, 146
Hammer ponds, 134
Hampton, 181
Hampton Court, 43; bridge, 181, 185; honour of, 43, 124, 181; railway station, 185
Hardman, 197
Hardwick, P.C., architect, (1792–1870), 150
Hascombe, 131
Haslemere, 138, 153
Hassel, John, artist, (1767–1825), 24
Hatchlands, 55
Hawksmoor, Nicholas, architect, (1666–1763), 80
Haxted Mill, 119
Headley Common, 100
Hearth, open, 13
Heathstone, 160, 165, 169
Heating, 13
Hedgecourt, iron industry at, 93
Henry, III, (1216–72), 29
Henry VI, steward of, 111
Henry VII, (1485–1509), 128
Henry VIII, (1509–47), 43, 115, 123, 124, 128
Hever, William de, 119
Hicks, Seymour, 110–11
High end, **12**, 13, 134
Hindhead, 142
Hip, 25, 64
Hoar Way, 17
Hog's Back, 21, 24, 26, 69, 156, 157, 166, 169
Holbein staircase, 87
Holland, Henry, architect, (1740–1806), 123
Hollar, 69
Holman, George, 93
Holman, Robert, 93
Holmbury St Mary, 77; Iron Age Fort, 205
Holmwood, 200
Hope, Thomas, 83–4; Hope diamond, 84
Horley, 114
Horne, James, architect, (d. 1756), 35
Horsell, 161–2
Horsell Common Preservation Society, 162
Horsham Slab, (slates, tiles), 45, 80, 93, 160, 193, 201, 205
Horsley Towers, **51**, 52
Howard, Charles, Duke of Norfolk, 83
Howard, Lord William, of Effingham, 87
Hull, Richard, 77
Hunt, Holman, O.M., artist, (1827–1910), 43
Hurtwood, 205

**Iron, wealden,** 93, 194; cast, 22, 115; furnace, 138; mill, 74; production methods, 133
Ironstone, 29, 79, 95, 165

**Jacobean,** 93
Jacobs Well, 42
James I, (1603–25), 29, 43, 123, 128
James, Capt. Edward Renouard, R.E., 17
Jekyll, Gertrude, gardener, (1843–1932), 21, 131
Jenkinson, Mr, 198
Jetty, 90, 175, 186, 205; continuous, 44, 63, 116, 138, 172, 194; crosswing, 73, 93, 95, 139, 153, 160; end, 169; gable, 65; internal, 62, 202; wealden, 96, 137
Johnson, P.M., architect, (1865–1936), 70
Jowl, **12,** 15, 24, 107

**Keats, John, poet, (1795–1821),** 199
Keep, 29, **29;** shell, 17
Kent, border, **2,** 96, 114
Kent, William, architect, (1684–1748), 80, 144, 146
Kew: Dutch house, 22
King, Lord, Baron Ockham, 52
Kingpost, 54, 176
Kingston Bypass, 147
King, William, Earl Lovelace, 52
Kitchen, detached, 17, 65, 73
Knaphill, 162
Knyvett, Lord Thomas, 172

**Laleham,** 172, 173
Lane, William, 190
Lap joint, 115, 213
Leather, 74
Leatherhead, 45; bridge, 45, 188, **189;** Bridge Street, 45; No. 33 Church Street, 47, **47;** The Mansion, 47; parish church, 47, 48; The Running Horse,

45, 47, 189; Wood Dene, 47
Leigh, 193–4
Leith Hill, 77, 197
Leopold, Prince of Saxe-Coburg, 146
Leoni, Giacomo, Palladian architect, (1686–1746), 55
Leptis Magna, 159
Lesenes, 30, 213
Levenson-Gower, family, 114
Limestone, 107, 111
Limnerslease, 26
Limpsfield, 95–6; 114; Dentillens Lane, **97**
Lingfield, 95, 116, **118,** 119–20
Little Bookham, 50
Littlefield Manor, 166
Littleton, nr Loseley, 27, 141, 149
Littleton Church, nr Shepperton, 179
London Necropolis and National Mausoleum Company, 163
Lordshill, 64
Loseley, 27, 149–50, **151**
Low end, 13
Loxwood, 131
Lutyens, Sir Edwin, O.M., K.C.I.E., P.R.A., architect, (1869–1944), 21, 154, 194, 207; bridge at Hampton Court, 181, 185; Goddards, 79; Littlecroft, 42; lych-gate, Shere, **72;** Millmead, 131; Moslem Burial Ground, 162; Red House, 50
Lynde family, 116
Lyne, 160

**M3,** 160, 173
M23, 105
Marlborough, Duchess of, 67
Manhood, Sussex, 197, 213
Mansard, François, architect, (1598–1666), 119
Marble. *See* Petworth *and* Purbeck
Mary I, (1553–8), 43
Mathematical tiles, 44, 80, 176, 198, 213

Maufe, Sir Edward, architect, (1883–1974), 42, 131
Mawbey, Sir Joseph, 160
Meredith, George, O.M., novelist, (1828–1909), 178, 199
Merstham, 110; church, 104, 105; Quality Street, **109**
Merstham stone, 103, 104, 213
Merton, 197
Mickleham, 190, 198; church, **199;** Juniper Hall, **196**
Middleton, Viscount, 41
Milford, 153
Millais, Sir John Everett, Bt., P.R.A., artist, (1829–96), 43
Mills: Byfleet, 124; Castle, Dorking, 190, **191;** Catteshall, Godalming, 141; Cosford, 154, **156;** Cobham, 186; Elstead, 141; fulling, 30; Gomshall, 74; gunpowder, 66, 67; Haxted, 116, **117,** 119; iron, Abinger Hammer, 74; Newark, 128; Ockham, 127; Outwood, 122, **122;** paper, 66; Pippbrook, 81; Pixham, 83, 190; Rickford, 165; Shalford, **60,** 61; Town, Guildford, 40
Milton, 80
Minstrel gallery, 120
Moat sites, 121, 123
Modillion, 115, 213
Mole, 47, 80, 123, 181, 185; swallows, 189
Monmouth, Duke of, 34, 99
Monson, Lord, 111
Moon, James, 150
Moorhouse Bank, **2,** 96
Moorhouse, James, monumental mason, (fl. 1750s), 61
Moor Park, 22
More, Sir William, 149
More-Molyneux, Sir William, 150; wife, 150
Morris, William, artist-designer, (1834–

96), 89
Mortice and tenon, 115, 213
Motte, 17, 100
Moulding, dogtooth, 30, 211

**Nelson, Viscount Horatio, (1758–1805),** 199
Newark Priory, 67, **126,** 127, 128
Newdigate, 194–5; Greens Farm, **195**
Norbury Park, 190, 198
Norbury, Sir John, 187

**Oaks Park,** 99
Oakwood: church, 202; Pollingfold, 202, **203**
Oakwood Hill, 201, 202
Oatlands, 43
Ockham Park, 52; church, 71; mill, 127
Ockley, 197, 200–201
Ogee, 214. *See also* Brace
Old Woking, 127, 128, 129, 130; Old Brew House, **130;** Old Manor House, **129,** palace, **128;** Wey Cottage, Lea Cottage, church, **129**
Onslow family, 55
Ordnance survey, 17
Oriel, 83, 150, 201, 214
*Orné,* 61, 89, 201, 214
Outshot, 25, 214
Outwood, 122; mill, **122**
Oven, communion bread, 96; domestic, 205
Oxenford, 154. *See also* Peper Harow
Oxted, 94–5; Bell Inn, 94

**Pachesham,** 188; cottage, **188**
Paine, James, architect, (1716–89), 160, 179
Painting, church, 30, 95, 105, 153
Palladian, 55, 56, 83, 87, 146, 160, 181, 214
Palladio, Andrea, architect, (1518–80), 214

Pantry, **12,** 50, 62
Paper manufacture, 66
Papercourt, 128
Parclose. *See* SCREEN
Parker, Eric, (1870–1955), 29
Parlour, 12, 13, 62, 141, 179
Parsons, Sir John, 87
Passengers Farm, 166
Pastorini, Benedict, artist, (fl. 1770s), 190
Patching, Resta, 83
Peacock, Thomas Love, poet, (1785–1866), 178
Peak, Henry, architect, (1832–1914), 30
Pearson, J.L., architect, (1817–97), 89, 114, 123
Pelham, Henry, 144
Peper Harow, 141; granary, **142**
Pepys, S., F.R.S., (1633–1703), 36
Perkins, Sir William, 176
Peter the Great of Russia, 150
Petworth, 134
Petworth marble, 30, 71, 73, 214
Pews, 137
Pigsty, 134
Pilaster, 30, 214. *See also* LESENES
Pilgrims, 17, 67, 69
Pilgrims' Hall, Winchester, 121
Pilgrims' Way, 17, 69, 107
Pirbright, 157, 163, 165; church, **163**
Pitch Place, 166
Pitt, William, stateman, (1759–1806), 198
Pixham. *See* DORKING *and* MILLS
Plague, 43
Plan, house, **12,** 13
Polesden Lacy, **49,** 50
Porch, 71, 127, 163
Portsmouth, 131; road, 143, 144, 146, 149
Pre-Christian, 95
Pre-Raphaelite, 43, 190
Prince Regent, 30

Principal post, 15, 107, 214
Prinkham. *See* STERBOROUGH CASTLE
Processions, 48, 95
Prosser, Henry, local artist, 30
Puddingstone, 133, 160, 214
Pugin, A.W.N., architect, (1812–52), 69, 141
Pulborough, 197
Pulpit, 127, 143, 163, 176
Purbeck marble, 172
Puttenden Manor, 116
Puttenham, 23, 24, 26; priory, **24;** 58
The Street, **23**
Pyrford, 127, 128; church, **127**

**Queen struts, 12**
Quenell, Peter, 138
Quenell, Robert, 138

**Racing:** Derby Week, 99; motor, 124
Rafters, butted common, **12,** 13, 15; common, **12;** principal, **12, 15;** reducing, **12,** 15
Railway, 40
Raised eaves, 66, 206
Ralegh, Sir Walter, (1552–1618), 54
Randyll, Sir Edward, 67
Randyll, Morgan, 67
Randyll, Vincent, 67
Ranmore, 80; St Barnabas, **80**
Rede, John, 115
Redhill, 88–9, 115
Reeves, Edward, builder, 176
Refronting, 182. *See also* BRICK
Reigate, 87, 88, 104; Brownes Lodge, **88;**
Town Hall, **86**
Rennie, John, F.R.S., architect, engineer, (1761–1821), 171
Re-used timber, 205
Ripley, 147, 149; The Anchor, **147;** Main Street, **148**
Rodney, Admiral, (1719–92), 179

Roman: Roads: Devil's Highway, 159;
Stane Street, 13, 81, 93, 96, 103, 189;
temple, 206; villa, 103
Romanesque font, 103
Rood, 95, 127 *See also* SCREEN
Roof structures, 15
Roubiliac, L.F., sculptor, (1695–1762), 181
Rowhook, 197, 202
Royal Horticultural Society Gardens, 124
R.S.P.C.A., Millbrook Centre, 160
Ruckmans, 201
Ruskin, John, artist, critic, (1819–1900), 190
Runnymede, 171

**St Augustine, Canons Regular of the Order of,** 115
St Catherine's, 27, 67, 149
St Martha and All Holy Martyrs, 69
St Martha's Chapel, 67
St Thomas the Martyr, Aldebury. *See* NEWARK PRIORY
Salvation Army, 181
Sandby, Paul, (1725–1809), 158
Sandby, Thomas, (1721–98), 158–9, 190
Sandes, Beatrice de, 128
Sandhills, 154
Sandown Park, 185
Sandstone, 77, 95, 107, 115
Saxon, 30, 48, 69, 70, 79, 187, 193;
bishop, 70; consecration cross, 70;
motte, 100; window, 153, 154
Scissor braces, 15
Scott, Sir George Gilbert, R.A., (1811–78), 80, 115
Scott, George Gilbert, jun., (1837–97), 88
Scott, Sir Giles Gilbert, R.A., (1880–1960), 150
Scratch dial, 131
Screen, 13; chancel, 176; parclose, 113;

rood, 95, 127
Screens passage. *See* CROSS PASSAGE
Seale, 22, 23
Send, 127, 130
Service end, 13, 62, 134, 141, 179
Shalford, 61, 62, 138; mill, 60; park, 27
Shamley Green, 62, 64, 65, 66, 131, 202;
Barnett Farm, **66;** Watts Cottage, **65**
Shannon, Viscount, monument, 181, **183**
Shaw, Norman, architect, (1831–1912), 21, 100; The Hallams, 206, **207;**
Merrist Wood, **164,** 165; Pierrepont, 142; Rectory Place, Guildford, 42;
style of, 108, 111, 194
Shepard, Ernest, illustrator, (1879–1976) 61
Shepherd, Rev. H., 105
Shepperton, 176, 178
Shere, 67, 72, 73, 74; village, **72**
Sheridan, Rt. Hon. Richard Brinsley, (1751–1816), 50
Shingles, 48, 73, 96, 115, 120, 135, 137, 163
Shoelands, 23
Sidlow Bridge, 193
Sidney Wood. *See* ALFOLD
Silent Pool, 70
Skelton, 189
Slyfield, 54, 61
Smallfield Place, 121–2
Smithwood Common, 131; Little Pittance, **132**
Smoke bay, 15, 64, 130, 162–3, 166, 169, 188, 194
Smoke chamber, 163
Smoke: deflector, 64, 137; deposits, 64
Snower Hill, 193
Soane, Sir John, R.A., architect, (1753–1837), 69, 146
Somers, painter, (fl. 1739), 150
Sondes family, 116
South Downs, 197

Spere, 13, 215
Spire, 150; brooch, 73; shingled, 115, 120, 135, 137
Sprocket, **12**
Staines, 157, 171, 172
Stair, 23, 35, 59, 61, 188; newel, 116, 144; turret, 15, 131
Stane. *See* ROMAN ROADS
Stanwell, 172; church, **170**
Sterborough Castle, 119
Stoke D'Abernon, 187; church, **187**
Stone, Nicholas, sculptor, (1586–1647), 172
Street, G.E., architect, (1824–81), 77, 99
Sunbury, 181
Suppression of monasteries, 22
Surrey Militia, 99
Sussex border, 114, 201
Sussex marble. *See* PETWORTH MARBLE
Sutton: Fulvens Farm, 77
Sutton Place, 127, 131, 149
Swallows. *See* MOLE
Swallow Tile Works, 202, **205**

**Tadworth Court,** 100, **101**
Talleyrand-Perigord, Prince, (1754–1838), 198
Tandridge, 114, 115
Tanneries, 74
Tarn, E. Wyndham, architect, (fl. 1860s), 21
Tatsfield, 113
Tattenham Corner, 100
Temple, Rt. Hon. Sir William, Bt., statesman, author, (1628–99), 22
Tenon. *See* MORTICE
Terries, Ellaline, actress, 110
Teulon, S.S., architect, (1812–73), 172, 181

Thames Ditton, 181–2
Thames, River, 123, 178
Thatch, 107, 169
Thorncombe Street, 131
Thorpe, 159–60
Thorpe, John, 93
Thursley, 154; Hill Farm, **155**
Tie beam, **12**; 24
Tile hanging, 61, 90, 135, 137, 187, 193, 194, 200, 201
Tilford, 141
Tillingbourne Stream, 61, 67, 70, 73, 74
Tithe map, 70
Titsey, 114
Toll-gates, 143
Tonbridge, Richard de, 69
Transitional style, 30, 73, 96, 215, 216
Transverse bracing, 15. *See also* BRACE
Trouts Farm, 200
Tupper, Martin, author, (1810–89), 71
Turner, J.M.W., R.A., artist, (1775–1851), 179
Turner, Thackeray, architect, (fl. 1894–1913), 42, 141
Turnpike, 26, 143
Tuscan columns, 44, 137

**Unstead,** 139, **139**; upper, 139
Unsworth, W.F., architect, (fl. 1889–93), 162

**Vanbrugh, Sir John, architect, dramatist, (1664–1726),** 144–5
Verio, Antonio, artist, (c. 1640–1707), 87
Villiers, Barbara, Duchess of Cleveland, 43
Virginia Water, 158–9; ruins, **158**
Voysey, C.F.A., architect, (1857–

1941), 42

**Wall paintings.** *See* PAINTINGS
Wallplate, **12;** second wallplate, 66
Walton, 179–81; church, **180**
Walton on the Hill, 100, 103
Wanborough, 24, 25; barn, **25**
Ware, Isaac, architect, (d. 1776), 45
Warenne, William de, 87
Watson, J.B., architect, (1803–81), 172
Watts, G.F., R.A., O.M., artist, (1817–1904), 26; chapel, **26**
Waverley Abbey, **20,** 21, 24, 139, 141
Waylands Farm, 185
Waynflete. *See* WINCHESTER
Weald, 13, 89, 113, 115, 193, 197, 200, 202
Wealden clay, 114
Wealden house, **72,** 73, 96, 120, 137; modern, 116; probable, 62
Wealden iron. *See* IRON
Weatherboarding: church, 48; house, 20, 44, 107, 182; mill, 61, 119
Webb, Philip, architect, (1831–1915), 62
Wellingtonias, 200
Wells, H.G., novelist, (1866–1946), 162
Wessels, Leonard, 100
West Byfleet. *See* BYFLEET
West Clandon, 55; church, **56;** Clandon Park, **57**
Westcott, 80
West Horsley, 54, 55; Old Cottage, **53**
West Humble, 80; Camilla Lacy, 198
Westminster, 127; hall, 121
West Molesey, 185
Weston Green, 182
Weston, Sir Richard, 131, 149
Weston Street, 69
Weybridge, 123

Wey, River, 21, 27, 29, 67, 123, 127, 138; bridges, 138–9, 150; Eashing, **140**
Whipley Manor, 131, 166
Whiteley village, 185
Wilkins, William, R.A., architect (1778–1839), 69
Winchester, Bishops of, 73; Henry de Blois, 17; William Gifford, 21; William Waynflete, 17, 144
Windbrace, **12**
Windlesham, 169
Windows: cast iron casement, 152; Saxon, 153, 154
Windsor Great Park, 158
Winkworth Farm, 131
Winterfold Hill, 197, 206
Wisley, 124, 127
Witley, 153–4; Step Cottages, **153**
Woburn Hill, 123
Woking, 127. *See also* HORSELL *and* OLD WOKING
Wonersh, 62, 64, 65; Dower House, **64;** Grantley Arms, **63**
Woodcote, 45
Wood Street, 166
Woodyer, Henry, architect, (1816–96), 24, 61, 80, 81, 84, 87, 124
Worcester Park Farm, 43
Worplesdon, 42, 165–6; Merrist Wood, **164;** Whites Farm, **167**
Wotton, 79–80, 202; church, **79**
Wren, Sir Christopher, F.R.S., architect, (1632–1723), 104, 120
Wyatt, Richard, 150
Wyatt, T.H., architect, (1807–80), 123
Wyattville, Sir Jeffry, (1766–1840), 159

**York, Frederick Duke of,** 123

**Zouch, Sir Edward,** 129